Dublin

D0826900

- A ☞ in the text denotes a highly recommended sight
- A complete A–Z of practical information starts on p.104
- Extensive mapping on cover flaps

Berlitz Publishing Company, Inc.

Princeton   Mexico City   Dublin   Eschborn   Singapore

Text:	Jack Messenger and Brigitte Lee
Editors:	Donald Greig, Delphine Verroest
Photography:	Pete Bennett
Layout:	Media Content Marketing, Inc.
Cartography:	Visual Image

Thanks to Dublin Tourism and Board Fáilte for their invaluable help in the preparation of this guide.

Found an error we should know about? Our editor would be happy to hear from you, and a postcard would do. Although we make every effort to ensure the accuracy of all the information in this book, changes do occur.

Cover photograph: *O'Connell Street*

ISBN 2-8315-6415-8
Revised 1997 – First Printing October 1997

Printed in Switzerland by Weber SA, Bienne
019/710 REV

CONTENTS

DUBLIN

DUBLIN AND
THE DUBLINERS

There are many Dublins. It is a city of myth and legend, history and upheaval, a city imagined and reimagined, invented and appraised, described and depicted in the literature and art of its sons and daughters down the centuries. Home to over one million people, and boasting some of the world's most harmonious architecture, it provides hospitality that is proverbial. Yet it is difficult to think of any other city that is so much a part of the imagination of its inhabitants and its artists. Dublin has many layers, and part of the excitement of visiting is learning to discover them all for yourself.

Dublin is a city of moods. There is the quiet, elegant, restrained Dublin of Fitzwilliam and Merrion Squares and there is rush-hour Dublin, when half the city seems bent on swapping places with the other half. There is the bourgeois Dublin of Grafton Street and Bewley's Oriental Café, and then there is "South Bank" Dublin, home and workshop to numerous artists. The occasional cry of gulls and an unexpected distant vista will remind you that Dublin is by the sea and the mountains, but there is also the Dublin of wide boulevards, green parks, and gardens. Most important of all, perhaps, there is a Dublin for every visitor the city welcomes.

City on the Liffey

"Anna Livia," as the River Liffey is known, flows from west to east through the centre of the city to Dublin Bay. The river forms a natural line between the north and south of the city. Historically and culturally this north-south distinction has always been important, and still is today, with a dose of good-humoured rivalry between the two areas. Farther north and south are the sweeping curves of the Royal and Grand Canals,

Nowhere is the warm Irish welcome more in evidence than in a traditional pub.

while visible from all parts of the capital are the Dublin and Wicklow Mountains, which hold Dublin tight to the coast.

This geography is important in understanding Dublin, for it has always been a special part of Ireland — in the 17th and 18th centuries it was for many a city of privilege and power while the people in the surrounding countryside lived in the most terrible hardship. By virtue of invasion and settlement of one kind or another, Dublin has long belonged politically to Europe, absorbing different peoples and sending her own sons and daughters to all parts of the world.

Dublin, with a population of more than a million, is yet an intimate city where everyone seems to know one another. This is very rare in the modern world, let alone in the capital city of a European nation. This individuality of the people and their city perhaps explains the legendary hospitality of many Dubliners. They are keen to know you and involve you in social events. There is less of the anonymity and standardization seen in so many other cities. Multinational firms and chains have made far fewer inroads here than elsewhere, though of course in the main shopping streets you will recognize famous names. Many shops, hotels, and guesthouses have been owned and managed by the same families for years, and theirs is the welcome of traditional Dublin hospitality.

Dublin has always had the power to attract and beguile its visitors. It is a cultured city, with great artistic vitality. It is the only city to have produced three Nobel Prize winners for Literature — Yeats, Shaw, and Beckett. Joyce, the high priest of literary modernism, imagined and interpreted Dublin for the world in his novel *Ulysses* (you'll see reminders of this everywhere you go).

However, it is as if the city produces artists of this stature by accident, even against its will. Beckett and Joyce, like so many of the Irish people, had to leave their homeland in order to understand it and work as they wished.

Dublin is at the center of a tremendously vibrant popular culture of storytellers, myth-makers, and musicians who, through thick and thin down the centuries, have survived and flourished — many of them can be met at any pub on a Saturday night. A traditional evening of live music, storytelling, and traditional dance is a wonderful introduction to this side of Irish life and a "must" for any visitor.

Light and Rain

The Dublin climate can best be described as "changeable" and you should be prepared for some rain. Yet the sudden shifts from light to dark, sunshine to shower, are part of the magic of the city and can alter your perceptions of the place. The buildings seem to transform themselves depending on the light — a good excuse, if one were needed, to tour the city more than once. Dublin under a lowering sky is a different place from Dublin in sunshine. If there is a shower you can always shelter in one of the excellent pubs or cafés found all across the city.

In the past, it would have been possible to wax lyrical about Dublin but almost have to apologize for the quality

Ha'penny Bridge, a cast-iron rainbow across the Liffy in Ireland's capital of music.

of food offered in its restaurants and cafés. Fortunately, all that has changed. There has been a quiet revolution in eating habits as people have come to appreciate and exploit fully the quality of fresh Irish produce. New Irish cuisine has been the result, and it is to be thoroughly recommended. All types of international cuisines are available, many offering excellent quality and value for the money. For the traditionally minded, the full Irish breakfast is still going strong; imagine an enormous fry-up and then double it, and you'll have some idea of what it involves. If you eat it all you'll be able to skip lunch.

Dublin is eminently walkable. Many of the major attractions are centrally located and can be reached on foot, even from suburban areas. The main shopping area of Grafton Street is semi-pedestrianized. Dublin Tourism offers a number of self-guided walking tours.

College Green, the home of Trinity College (see page 26), provides a natural focus, as it is from there, at the north-west corner, that you can venture north of the River Liffey along O'Connell Street toward Parnell Square, west along the south bank through Temple Bar, and south toward St. Stephen's Green. Trinity College itself is a wealth of architectural interest and is the home of the beautiful and revered illuminated manuscript known as the Book of Kells.

There is no "metro" as such, but the DART (Dublin Area Rapid Transit) runs from north and south through the city and along the coast and is an ideal way to see outlying districts and villages. The bus service is also excellent, and there are many guided bus tours, of both Dublin itself and the surrounding countryside (see the Excursions chapter, page 69).

City and Countryside

Despite some taller modern buildings, Dublin is still a city of human proportions, thanks largely to the buildings of the 18th and early 19th centuries. Georgian Dublin is part of the city's glory, but it has often had a hard time surviving decay and the developers. However, things are changing, and the city retains a balance and charm that verges on gentility in areas like Ballsbridge.

Where do Dubliners go for their open spaces? In a city of such human proportions it is not surprising that parks and gardens abound for recreation and relaxation. Phoenix Park in the northwest is the largest open space, but squares like St. Stephen's Green are the garden oases of the city.

More elemental spaces are generously provided in Dublin's hinterland. On the coast, Sandymount and Dollymount Strands are the places to go — as many thousands of Dubliners do — if you fancy sea with your sun. Farther afield, the beautiful Wicklow Mountains provide more rugged countryside, occasionally studded with breathtaking houses and gardens like those of Castletown and Powerscourt. To the north and west are the ancient sites of Ireland, the evocative hill of Tara and the long barrows of Knowth and Newgrange.

Young at Heart?

With its universities and professional schools, Dublin is home to a large student population. The universities attract eager students from all over the country and indeed the world, and this influx adds spice to the city's social life. Young and old, stranger and Dubliner rub shoulders quite happily, and, as a consequence, in recent times there has been a relaxation of social attitudes. The city is also proud of its contribution to popular music: there is even a self-guided tour of the city to find the old haunts of U2, Bob Geldof, and Sinead O'Connor.

Whatever your age, whatever your outlook, there is a Dublin to suit everyone waiting to be discovered.

A BRIEF HISTORY

Ancient Ireland

The myths and legends of Irish oral tradition and literature — myths and legends that still exercise their power today — developed from the ancient mists of history. Thanks to the country's geographical remoteness, it was never conquered by the Romans. In the 4th and 5th centuries B.C., however, the Celts arrived (from where, nobody knows for sure), and it was they who decisively influenced the culture of Ireland.

Before Christianity came to these shores, Ireland was a series of sophisticated semi-independent kingdoms, each acknowledging the High King of Tara as their overlord (the Hill of Tara, to the north of Dublin, can be visited today). Such was the strength of the "nation" (if such a term can be used at this time) that it was the Irish who preyed on the Romans; legend has it that one of the captives they brought back with them was the future St. Patrick, patron saint of Ireland. It was St. Patrick who used the example of the shamrock to explain the Christian Trinity to King Laoghaire and an assembled crowd at Tara. The king was converted and the plant has been a symbol of Ireland ever since. A Christian settlement grew up around a ford on the River Liffey.

A Mission to Europe

The successful fusion of early Christianity with Celtic culture produced the golden age of Ireland, lasting from the 5th to the 12th century. It was during this time that Ireland became the light of the known world, sending out its learned teachers and monks all over Europe, and establishing itself as the Land of Saints and Scholars. The brilliance of learning and faith blazed in the gloom of the Dark Ages, and the influence and pervasiveness of Irish cultural zeal can still be seen today in the European towns and monastic orders bearing the names of Irish saints. The importance of this phase of Irish history, for both the Irish themselves and European civilization in general, cannot be underestimated.

Throughout this period Ireland was subject to repeated Viking attack and invasion, notably during the 9th and 10th centuries. The great centres of learning, the monastic libraries, were sacked, and what could not be removed was destroyed. It was also the Vikings, however, who established the first towns of Ireland, among them Dublin (the remains of the original Viking fort can be seen in Dublin Castle).

In A.D. 988 Irish kings fought for the city and won. The first Christ Church Cathedral was founded in 1038 and the Vikings were pushed back and to some extent absorbed. Their influence waned and was succeeded in the 12th century by the Anglo-Norman knights of King Henry II. Henry landed at Dublin, proclaimed himself Lord of Ireland, and was confirmed as such by the English Pope Adrian IV. It took less than two centuries for this first English incursion to be absorbed into Irish life, and this pattern of invasion and absorption was repeated throughout subsequent Irish history.

St. Audoen's, Dublin's sole medieval church, stands beside a section of the ancient city walls.

Henry granted a charter to Dublin in 1174, which gave the city rights to free trade, and in 1204 Dublin Castle became the centre of English administrative power. The city elected its first mayor in 1229, and parliament was held for the first time in 1297.

Beyond The Pale

As the immediate area around Dublin came to acknowledge the authority of the English Crown, it formed the basis of "The Pale," the area of English influence and control that was largely separate from the rest of (Celtic) Ireland. The rest of the country, however, sought opportunities for rebellion, but the set, traditional structure of semi-independent princedoms frustrated cohesive action.

In 1366, the English convened a parliament and passed the Statutes of Kilkenny, a series of laws which deprived the native Irish of all those rights outside English law. Persecution of Irish Catholics by Henry VIII led to the dissolution of the monasteries, and churches were either destroyed or given over to Protestants, which explains why Dublin's two cathedrals, Christ Church and St. Patrick's, are Protestant rather than Catholic.

Unrest and abortive rebellion characterized the 15th and 16th centuries, as a handful of Earls within The Pale held absolute power over large estates, while beyond it the country was in the hands of Gaelic clans. Rebellions against the rule of the English were put down ruthlessly.

The Irish, in effect deprived of their country, bravely fought on, but by 1607 were left leaderless by the "Flight of the Earls," in which the two Ulster earls O'Neill and O'Donnell went into exile on the Continent after yet another foiled rebellion. The granting of huge tracts of fertile land in Ulster (Northern Ireland) to Scottish settlers was the foundation for the troubles in the North today.

From Cromwell to the Boyne

The native Irish had been reduced to starvation by the time Oliver Cromwell arrived in Dublin in 1649, but his own campaigns in Ireland resulted in more than 600,000 Irish dead or deported. Those who remained were dispossessed still further, with the rich lands awarded to English settlers.

The old pattern repeated itself when these settlers came to think of themselves as Irish rather than English, while the native Irish they had dispossessed served on lands they themselves had once owned.

The Ascendancy, as the rich landowners were termed, lived lives of unrivalled luxury on their vast estates, while the rest of the country survived in utter poverty, deprived of food, education, and culture — and land.

At the Battle of the Boyne in 1690, the Irish fought for James II against the claimants to the English throne, Mary and William of Orange. The battle was lost, and the defeated army straggled into Dublin, after which James II fled to France. The Earl of Lucan reorganized the army so successfully that King William was forced to make concessions on religious freedom and Irish rights. The agreement was reneged upon, however, and the English parliament enacted instead the Penal Laws of 1704, which intensified the poverty throughout the country.

At home, resistance took the form of underground movements and the cultivation of traditional Irish gifts of song and storytelling. The Ascendancy, jealous of their privileges, resisted any change to the status quo. In 1782 the first Irish parliament was formed in Dublin, largely through the energies of Henry Grattan, MP for the city.

A violent Protestant sectarian backlash was provoked by the repeal of Penal Laws in the 1790s, in response to the nonsectarian movement led by Wolfe Tone and others for the freedom of the Irish people. Tone sought aid from France, but the fleets sent to Ireland were scattered by bad weather and arrived too late. Tone was captured and either was murdered or committed suicide.

Dublin's importance grew dramatically as the city became the centre of social and business life in Ireland. The architecture stems largely from this period. The glory of this lively and cosmopolitan city lasted until 1801, when the Act of Union brought Ireland under direct rule from London. Quite suddenly, building stopped, the rich and powerful left for England, and the city became just a provincial capital in a state of long, slow decline.

The Union and O'Connell

The new government, made up only of "suitable people," resulted in 1803 in yet another rebellion, led by the great Irish hero Robert Emmet. Twenty years later Daniel O'-Connell formed the peaceful but powerful Catholic Association, and in 1829 the Duke of Wellington, in a bid to avoid a civil war, passed the Catholic Emancipation Bill (allowing Irish Catholics to go to the Westminster parliament for the first time ever). O'Connell was made lord mayor of Dublin in 1841, but failed in his bid to have the Act of Union repealed and an Irish parliament reestablished, not least because by then the Great Famine in Ireland was altering political priorities.

Famine and Home Rule

This particular famine took the form of a blight on the staple food, the potato. It first struck in 1845 and it is estimated that more than one million people died and that a similar number emigrated to escape the ravages of the catastrophe. By the end of the 1800s the population of the country was virtually halved.

Hope survived, however: the nationalist movement known as Young Ireland was defeated, but it bequeathed to the country an example of Protestants and Catholics working together for freedom. This combination of "orange" and "green" gave Ireland its tricolour national flag.

The demand for home rule for Ireland was led by an Irish Member of Parliament, the charismatic Charles Stewart Parnell. For a time, it looked as if the campaign was going to succeed, but the murder of two British politicians by a secret organization and the citing of Parnell himself as co-respondent in a scandalous divorce case led many to withdraw their support.

The Bill for Home Rule became law just as World War I broke out, but with the proviso that it was not to be enacted until hostilities ended.

In the meantime the Ulster Volunteers (supporters of union with Britain) and the Irish Volunteers (set up specifically to oppose them) were formed: the seeds of Ireland's further troubled history had germinated.

Easter Rising and War

Two years into World War I, on Easter Monday, 24 April 1916, what became known as the Easter Rising took place in the streets of Dublin. The Irish Volunteers, their ranks swelled by the Citizen's Army led by Patrick Pearse, took control of a number of key buildings in the capital. A Declaration of Independence was read out, and the Irish people were urged to fight. To the Dubliners it all seemed rather unreal, until fighting in the streets started with thousands of British troops.

More than 200 people were killed and many buildings destroyed before the Rising was put down. The execution of 15 of the leaders made martyrs of them all. One of the leaders,

Eamon De Valera (an American citizen), was imprisoned rather than killed — he later went on to become president of the 1919 Dublin parliament, which proclaimed a Declaration of Independence.

The whole episode of the Rising and the retribution that followed galvanized the Irish. In the general election of 1919 they returned to parliament an overwhelming number of Republicans; among them was the first woman ever to be elected an MP, Constance Gore-Booth.

A feared and brutal security force known as the Black and Tans (the colours

An exile in his lifetime, James Joyce now wanders the city like a latter-day Ulysses.

of its uniform) was dispatched to Ireland by the British government to try and pacify the country. The Anglo-Irish War resulted in a partial victory for Ireland, and in 1921 the Partition Act enabled the six counties of Northern Ireland to remain in the union with Britain, while the remaining 26 became independent. In the following year, however, a civil war broke out between those who supported Eamon De Valera and the treaty he signed with the British and those who did not.

The civil war lasted a year, and in 1922 the Irish Free State was born. In 1937 De Valera, still going strong, constructed a republican constitution for the country which took Ireland out of the British Commonwealth. The first president of the new republic was Douglas Hyde, who was inaugurated in 1938. During World War II, bombs from German planes fell twice on Dublin, but the country remained neutral.

For many years after its independence Ireland was characterized by a parochial and narrow-minded approach to its affairs, perhaps as an understandable result of the years of neglect and conquest. Since then, it has gradually taken its place on the world stage and adopted a more outward-looking stance. It was admitted into the United Nations in 1955 and the European Community in 1972. In 1988 the millennium celebrations of Dublin as an Irish city involved the restoration of many fine buildings and the erection of statues and monuments. A year before the celebrations, Dublin elected its first woman mayor, and in 1990 Ireland chose Mary Robinson as its first woman president. The ultimate accolade to the city's architectural and cultural attractions came in 1991, when it was designated European City of Culture.

The City Today

The years of Anglo-Irish privilege help explain the lingering resentment (in the 1960s and 1970s particularly) towards the architectural heritage from that period: the fine buildings are symbols of an oppressed past. Many did not escape the bulldozer and were razed to make way for brutalist modern developments; others are in a shockingly neglected state.

The centuries of foreign rule say something about the value placed on traditional culture and the individuality of the Dublin temperament. What is miraculous is that so much national suffering has not led to a bitter and suspicious attitude to strangers. On the contrary, the warm Dublin welcome continues to delight and amaze, and every visitor leaves with a lasting impression of the city's wit, grace, and charm.

HISTORICAL CHRONOLOGY

8000 B.C.	First evidence of human habitation in Ireland.
A.D. 432	St. Patrick brings Christianity to Dublin.
841	The Vikings build a fort on the Liffey.
1014	Brian Boru defeats the Vikings at the Battle of Clontarf.
1038	Christ Church established.
1162	Norman invasion.
1171	Henry II lands at Dublin.
1204	Anglo-Normans rule from Dublin Castle.
1297	Dublin's first parliament created.
1534	Catholic suppression under Henry VIII.
1592	Foundation of Trinity College granted by Elizabeth I.
1649	Irish rebellion put down by Oliver Cromwell.
1791	Wolfe Tone's rebellion.
1803	Robert Emmet's rebellion.
1829	Daniel O'Connell emerges as a leader; Catholic Emancipation Act passed by the Duke of Wellington.
1841	O'Connell made mayor of Dublin.
1845	Ireland's Great Famine strikes.
1867	Fenian rebellion put down.
1916	Easter Rising.
1919	Dublin parliament proclaims a Declaration of Independence; provisional government follows.
1919-1921	Ireland at war with Britain.
1922	Outbreak of Irish Civil War.
1927	First general election.
1937	Irish constitution adopted.
1938	First president, Douglas Hyde, elected.
1939-1945	Dublin bombed by Germany; Ireland remains neutral.
1955	Ireland joins the United Nations.
1972	Ireland joins the European Community.
1990	Ireland elects its first female president, Mary Robinson.
1991	Dublin designated European City of Culture.

WHERE TO GO

Dublin is a relatively compact city, and many of the places you will wish to see are within easy walking distance of one another. To absorb the atmosphere of the city and to really appreciate its architecture and gardens, walking is by far the best option (Sundays are particularly pleasant, when the city is comparatively free of traffic). However, there is also an excellent bus service; Dublin buses are efficiently run and venture out to several excursion destinations.

The best thing to do if you plan to use the buses is buy a complete book of timetables from the Dublin Bus office in Upper O'Connell Street (opposite the Tourist Information Office). The DART (railway) will also take you north and south along the coast. Car rental is quite expensive and is an unattractive and unnecessary option in a city of busy traffic and attendant parking problems, though you may wish to use a car to explore places well outside the city (see Excursions on pages 69–81). There are, however, many bus tours to outlying destinations.

A good orientation exercise is to start with an organized sightseeing tour — by bus, with either *Dublin Bus* from Upper O'Connell Street or *Bus Eireann* from the Travel Centre at Busaras in Store Street. Alternatively, you may prefer a tour in a horse-drawn hansom cab from St. Stephen's Green. There are no tours provided on the canals, but there are some on the rivers.

Your first port of call, depending on where you are staying, should be one of the city's tourist information centres. **Dublin Tourism** has one office at 14 Upper O'Connell Street (8:00 A.M.–8:00 P.M. Monday-Saturday in summer) and in the former St. Andrew's Church, Grafton Street.

There is also an information centre in the offices of **Bord Fàilte** (the Irish Tourist Board) at Baggot Street Bridge (9:15 A.M.–5:15 P.M. Monday-Friday). There you'll find maps, leaflets, and other useful information, and you can also arrange accommodation. In addition, Dublin Tourism has devised and signposted three self-guided walking tours of the city, which you can follow using the booklets provided.

AROUND GRAFTON STREET

Grafton Street, south of the river, is one of the main shopping streets of Dublin, along with O'Connell Street north of the river. This crowded, semi-pedestrianized thoroughfare is a pleasure to stroll down, with buskers and other entertainers performing in front of department stores such as **Brown Thomas**, and at no. 78, old **Bewley's Oriental Café**, which after 100 years has become something of an in-stitution in Dublin (get there early to see Dubliners reading the *Irish Times* over their breakfast-time black pud-ding). Of the eight branches in the city, this is historically the best: the windows to the rear of its faded art deco ground floor were designed by the stained-glass artist Harry Clarke. There is also a museum and theatre.

For stylish shopping, simply follow the crowds and you'll soon come to Grafton Street.

There are a number of more recent shopping com-plexes set around the Grafton Street area, probably the most impressive of which is the

DUBLIN HIGHLIGHTS

(See also Museum Highlights on page 59)

Casino at Marino: *Malahide Road, Marino, Dublin 3*. Lord Charlemont's 18th-century villa, one of Europe's finest buildings of the period. June–September daily 9:30am-6:30pm, October–May Wednesdays, Sundays noon-4pm. IR£2, children IR£1. (See page 77.)

Christ Church Cathedral: *Christchurch Place, Dublin 8*. Dublin's oldest building, standing on the site of an 11th-century church, with impressive stonework, tombs, and a vaulted crypt. (See page 47.)

Dublin Castle: *Palace Street, Dublin 2*. The city's former defence post, once the centre of British military power, and now home to an array of treasures. Monday–Friday for half-hour guided tours, 10am-12:15pm, 2-5pm; Saturday–Sunday 2-5pm. IR£1.75, children IR£1. (See page 45.)

Grafton Street: Join in with the buskers and shoppers, or pop into Bewley's Oriental Café. (See page 137.)

Merrion Square: One of the city's finest squares, dating from the mid-18th century, now the site of the National Gallery and previously home to Oscar Wilde and W.B. Yeats. (See page 53.)

O'Connell Street: Stroll down Dublin's grand boulevard, where every building and statue has a story to tell. Here lies the General Post Office in which history was made in 1916, when Connolly and Pearse proclaimed the Republic. (See page 37.)

St. Patrick's Cathedral: *Patrick's Close, Patrick Street, Dublin 8*. The national cathedral of the Church of Ireland, the oldest Christian site in Dublin. Suggested donation IR£1.0. (See page 51.)

St. Stephen's Green: Dating from medieval times, the oldest green in Dublin, a massive stretch of lawns and lovely gardens in the heart of the city. (See page29.)

Trinity College: *College Green, Dublin 2*. Founded in 1592, the university is now one of the main cultural and social hubs of the city. Its Colonnades Gallery houses the famous Book of Kells, and graduates include Bram Stoker and Samuel Beckett. 9:30am-5:30pm, Sunday 12-5pm; Old Library IR£3, Dublin Experience audio-visual and exhibition IR£2.75, combined ticket IR£5.00, concessions; half-hour guided tours (IR£3.50) include the Old Library but not the Dublin Experience. (See page 26.)

Powerscourt Townhouse Centre (an ornate clock points the way left just beyond Bewley's to the Clarendon Street entrance).

This 1770s mansion was formerly the residence of viscount Powerscourt and still possesses some magnificent plasterwork, particularly in the rear exit hall. The building has been tastefully converted, with a pleasant glass-roofed central courtyard with lots of balconies. There are many excellent cafés and restaurants, and you can shop on the various levels for antiques, crafts, and clothes. At the top is an exhibition gallery run by the Crafts Council of Ireland, which shows inspired iconoclastic crafts. In the summer months there is a programme of lunchtime recitals.

Next to the shopping centre, in South William Street, is the small and eclectic **Dublin Civic Museum** (see page 60), an unassuming museum of Dublin life over the years.

At the top of Grafton Street, where it meets the busy Nassau Street, you will see Jean Rynhart's statue of **Molly Malone**, 18th-century barrow girl and subject of a well-known tragic ballad. Erected in 1988 to celebrate Dublin's millennium as a city, it has become known as the "Tart with the Cart" to irreverent Dubliners!

Across the road from the statue and facing each other across College Street are Trinity College and the Bank of Ireland building. The **Bank of Ireland**, built in 1729 to house the Irish parliament, is really a series of additions to an original building, although the overall effect is one of elegance and superb proportion (the Corinthian portico was in fact designed by James Gandon, who was also responsible for the Custom House on the north bank of the Liffey). Plans to house parliament here after Independence came to nothing, and Leinster House (in Kildare Street) was chosen instead.

You can visit the Bank on weekdays 10:00 A.M.–4:00 P.M. (Thursdays until 5:00 P.M.). The Irish oak-panelled and ta-

Trinity College, a green oasis of peace and refinement framed within elegant structures.

pestried room used to be the House of Lords — it's worth seeing. (The building is open from Monday to Wednesday and on Friday from 10:00 A.M.–4:00 P.M., Thursday from 10:00 A.M.–5:00 P.M.) On Tuesdays, you can follow a free, 35-minute historical tour of the old House of Lords chamber (departures at 10:30 A.M., 11:30 A.M., 1:45 P.M.; meet in the vestibule of the bureau de change). The commentary is both entertaining and informative.

Behind the bank in Foster Place is the intimate **Bank of Ireland Arts Centre**, which hosts a variety of exhibitions, plays, and concerts.

☛ Trinity College

Across the road is **Trinity College**. Founded in 1592 on the site of a former monastery, the university sits on the island of College Green, a delightful area of magnificent buildings and squares, surrounded by a sea of traffic. You are welcome to walk round College Green, but some of the buildings may be closed, depending on the time of year (from May to September there is an audio-visual exhibition here showing the history of Dublin).

The university itself is one of the geographical and social hubs of the city, attracting students of all creeds and nationalities from around the world. A plethora of famous graduates includes Samuel Beckett, Oliver Goldsmith, Bram Stoker, and Oscar Wilde; resistance heroes Robert Emmet and Wolf Tone also studied here.

Walk through the gates of the 100 meter (300 foot) high west front, designed by Theodore Jacobsen and built in 1752. The statues on either side are of Edmund Burke and Oliver Goldsmith and over the gate is the **Junior Common Room**.

Front Square and **Parliament Square**, a harmonious green dating from the 18th century, are surrounded by the Chapel, Dining Hall, Examination Hall, Reading Room, and the splendid Campanile. On your left the **Dining Hall**, designed by Richard Castle, has been falling down ever since it was finished in the 1740s and has undergone frequent rebuilding, particularly after a damaging fire in 1984. You can have lunch in this beautifully restored building, sitting at trestle tables while portraits of various luminaries gaze down at you. The **Buttery** in the basement serves (fairly basic) meals.

The late 18th-century **Chapel** displays some fine plasterwork by Michael Stapleton and dazzling stained-glass windows commemorating Graves, Usher, and Berkeley, together with a 20th-century organ in an 18th-century case.

Opposite, and from the same era, is the **Examination Hall**, which occasionally holds concerts when examinations are not in progress, but is otherwise rarely open to the public (look through the spy hole in the door!). The beautiful stucco ceiling is by Michael Stapleton again (also responsible for the ceilings in the Dublin Writers Museum; see page 60). The rather bizarre sarcophagus commemorates Provost Baldwin, perhaps because he left a substantial fortune to the university in 1758.

Among the paintings is a portrait of Archbishop James Usher, who donated the Book of Kells (see page 68) to the University Library. Both the Chapel and Examination Hall were designed by Sir William Chambers, the architect responsible for Charlemont House in Parnell Square (see page 36) and the Casino at Marino (see page 77).

The 30 meter (100 foot) high **Campanile**, built in 1853 — reputedly on the site of the original monastery bell tower — houses the university's own bells. It is impossible to miss the huge *Reclining Connected Forms* by Henry Moore in **Fellows' Square**, or Alexander Calder's *Cactus* behind the Old Library.

Architect Paul Koralek's **Berkeley Library** can't quite be ignored, either, though you may wish to pass over this anachronism of the 1960s in silence as you walk to **Library Square**. The eastern side of the square once housed Oliver Goldsmith's rooms (renovated in Victorian times; little of the 18th-century building remains).

The **Library** was opened in 1732 and takes the form of a single room, but what a room it is. The light falling from one hundred windows illuminates the complementary textures of wood and book in a barrel-ceilinged chamber 64 meters (209 feet) long, lined with the busts of scholars (including, once again, Usher). The vast collection of millions of books includes a Shakespeare folio. The colonnade below the library was originally open to the elements in order to protect the books from the damp, but in 1892 the columns were bricked in to make room for more books. Today this space also includes a shop, a gallery for exhibitions from the library, and **The Treasury**, which exhibits early Christian manuscripts — this area can become crowded. Displayed in the new **Colonnades Gallery** is the Book of Kells (see page 68).

Dawson and Kildare Streets

The **Provost's House** on the southwest corner of College Green was built in the late 18th century and is one of the finest houses in the city. The rooms inside are beautiful, but the building is not open to visitors.

From College Green head down **Nassau Street** (site of some interesting bookshops), then turn right into **Dawson Street**. Here you'll find more bookshops and another shopping complex, this one built on the site of the Royal Hibernian Hotel and naturally called the **Royal Hibernian Way**.

St. Anne's Church (facing Anne Street South) provides the setting for lunchtime concerts (look for the notices in the vestibule), while the newly refurbished **Royal Irish Academy**, at 19 Dawson Street, has a great collection of books and manuscripts. A few doors down is the charming **Mansion House**, the official residence of the Mayor of Dublin since 1715. The house was built in 1710 for one Joshua Dawson (an 18th-century property speculator), from whom the street takes its name. Right behind it is the **Round Room**, where in 1919 the Irish parliament adopted the Declaration of Independence. The building was constructed in 1821 in honour of King George IV's visit.

You can walk down Molesworth Street to reach **Kildare Street**, where you will see the entrance to **Leinster House**, now home to the Irish parliament. This building is believed by some to have provided the basis for the design of Washington's White House in the United States, which was the work of Irish architect James Hoban in 1870. To the left is the entrance to the **National Library** and to the right is the **National Museum** (see page 65). Tickets and advance notice are required for the reading rooms of the library; the more than half million items here are a vast archive of the nation. Exhibitions are often held in the splendid entrance hall.

Deane & Woodward, the architects responsible for the library and museum, also built the **Kildare Street Club**, in 1861. This marvellous Victorian-Gothic building is famous for the fanciful stone carvings around the base of its pillars (one pillar, reputedly depicting the club members, shows monkeys playing billiards).

The club itself was a bastion of the Ascendancy establishment (see page 16). The building now houses the **Heraldic Museum and Genealogical Office** (see page 61), which can be invaluable in tracing ancestors.

 ## St. Stephen's Green

At the bottom of Kildare Street is **St. Stephen's Green**, formerly an open common but enclosed in 1663 and now a 9-hectare (22-acre) green in the heart of the city surrounded by some beautiful buildings. It is the oldest green in Dublin, dating back to medieval times, although formally laid out as a public park only in 1880 by Lord Ardilaun, then chairman of the Guinness brewery. The ornate gardens within the green are many and various, with large, formal lawns, a lake, duckponds, a bandstand, and a children's playground.

Entering the park from St. Stephen's Green North you will come across the **Wolfe Tone** memorial opposite the famous Shelbourne Hotel (1824), and behind it a work entitled *Famine*, both by sculptor Edward Delaney. Facing St. Stephen's Green South is Marjorie Fitzgibbon's bust of **James Joyce**, and while working your way around the park, you will see the 1907 **Fusilier's Arch** at the Grafton Street corner.

The **St. Stephen's Green Shopping Complex**, at the south end of Grafton Street, has a pseudo-Victorian façade and was built in the 1980s. A light and airy place, it houses a wide selection of shops and stalls as well as a pub. Halfway down the west side of the green is the massive Georgian **Royal College of Surgeons**, built in 1806. Those chips in the stonework are not the results of carelessness but bullet holes from the 1916 Rising: the building was occupied by fighters led by Countess Markievicz, a bust of whom you may already have come across in the green.

One of the best-kept secrets in Dublin's squares is the lovely **Iveagh Gardens**, accessible from Clonmel Street via Harcourt Street. Designed really as series of pleasure gardens, they were opened to the public in 1991 and have recently been restored.

The Georgian curve of **Harcourt Street** (constructed in 1775) was once home to George Bernard Shaw (nos. 60-61). An outpost of the Dublin Writers Museum is at 33 Synge Street. The **Shaw Birthplace Museum** (see page 67) is marked by a plaque written by the great man himself and is a charming evocation of a small Dublin household of the period.

From here it is a short walk following the signs to the **Irish-Jewish Museum** in Walworth Road (see page 62), while just around the corner from the museum at 1a Lennox Street is the **Bretzel Bakery** — its bagels are not to be missed!

This whole area of Portobello is an interesting suburb of Victorian terraced housing on wide streets, and if you go further on to Rathmines across the canal, don't miss the recently restored **Church of Our Lady of Refuge** (Lower Rathmines Road, Dublin 6). Its noble dome dominates the skyline, but what impresses is the enormous interior and august Corinthian portico.

Reclining figures on St. Stephen's Green—a popular lunch venue for Dubliners.

On the left along St. Stephen's Green South there begins a fine array of buildings, the first of which is the **University Church**, a Byzantine creation built in 1853 at the instigation of Cardinal Henry Newman, then rector of University College. This strangely compelling building's highly decorated interior should be seen. The smell of incense is memorable, as are the enormous stairs to the pulpit.

Next door, numbers 85 and 86 comprise the exquisite **Newman House**, part of University College (guided tours every half hour from May to October 10:00 A.M.–5:00 P.M., Saturday 2:00–5:00 P.M., Sunday 11:00 A.M.–2:00 P.M.; during the winter by arrangement; closed Monday; entrance IR£2, children IR£1). The house has been partially restored; work will continue through the 1990s.

Number 85 dates from 1740 and contains some Rococo *tours de force* by the Francini brothers, who also worked on Tyrone House (see page 40). Their expertise can be seen at number 86 next door, but is for once overshadowed by the work of Robert West, which features an enormous flock of different species of birds in various poses.

James Joyce was a student here, and towards the end of his life the poet Gerard Manley Hopkins was a lecturer here: his room has been restored and can be seen on the guided tour, which begins with a 15-minute video presentation. There is a very pleasant terrace and in the basement is The Commons, which ranks among the best restaurants in Dublin. Just beyond Newman House is **Iveagh House**, home to the Irish government's Department of Foreign Affairs, but closed to the public. Both Newman House and Iveagh House were designed by Richard Castle.

Beyond Iveagh House in Earlsfort Terrace (to the right) is the **National Concert Hall**, of impressive proportions — it's a conversion of an old Examination Hall of University College. All sorts of concerts and shows are staged here throughout the year, as well as regular summer lunchtime concerts.

Back at the northeast corner of St. Stephen's Green, near the Shelbourne Hotel, you can turn right into **Merrion Row** to peer through the railings at the small **Huguenot Cemetery** (no entry to visitors). This dates back to 1693, when Calvinists fled to Dublin after the revocation of the Edict of Nantes in 1685. They brought with them their traditions, particularly their architectural and weaving skills, which greatly enriched their adopted city.

NORTH OF THE RIVER

Dublin north of the Liffey has both a unique atmosphere and, like the southern part of the city, some magnificent buildings (some would say the best) and museums and galleries.

Crossing **O'Connell Bridge** where the monument to O'Connell looks down at you, there are fine views along the river: the Custom House and Financial Services Centre are on the right and just visible is the roof of the Irish Life Cen-

The 18th-century Four Courts, on the River Liffey, houses the Supreme and High Courts.

tre; to the left is the equally splendid Four Courts. The bridge was built in 1790 and widened until it was almost square in 1880. It is difficult to know which direction to follow from here, but you can turn left along the quays of the north bank towards the Four Courts (about 1.5 km/1 mile). The delightful cast-iron **Ha'penny Bridge** at Wellington Quay joins Merchants" Arch with Liffey Street and was built in 1816. From its vicinity looking up river you can see the green-topped column of the smock windmill (the largest in Europe) in the Guinness brewery and the spire and green roof of St. Patrick's Cathedral. Christ Church will also loom into view, as will the Catholic St. Audoen's; and no, you're not having a vision, that really is a statue of a blue- and white-robed Jesus blessing you from a rooftop corner.

O'Connell looks down on his very own bridge, which offers fine views over the Liffey.

On the corner of Liffey Street you'll see the sculpture known as "the hags with the bags." Two doors down from the bridge, next door to the woollen mills, is **The Winding Stair** bookshop and café, which is worth a browse.

The **Four Courts** was designed by James Gandon in 1785 after the death of the original architect. As one looks up from the magnificent Corinthian portico to the statues on the roof and the distinctive dome beyond, the building is an impressive sight. It contains the various courts of the city together with a library of law and a basement restaurant. The Four Courts was damaged in the fighting of the 1920s and a terrific fire destroyed all the official archives, but restoration work (in 1932) has removed nearly all traces of the destruction. You can see inside when the courts are in session.

Father Matthew Bridge, at the far end of Inns Quay, stands on the site of the first bridge in the city, which was built in 1214.

It is worth walking on to the pedestrianized areas of **Henry Street** and **Moore Street**, to see and hear their famous markets (you are, after all, in the city of Molly Malone). Expect some ribald remarks in broad Dublin accents from the stallholders. As a contrast to a traditional Dublin market, you can visit the **ILAC Centre** in Henry Street, a shopping mall with two department stores, a chapel, and a library (the latter holds regular exhibitions and displays and is worth seeing).

Beyond the Four Courts to the right is Church Street, with the church in question — **St. Michan's** — on the left. One of the oldest churches in Dublin, it was built in the 17th century on the site of a Danish chapel, but heavily restored in the 19th century. Handel is believed to have composed *The Messiah* here and the font was once graced by the infant Duke of Wellington. The church's chief claim to fame, however, is its vaults, which, because of their characteristic geology, have preserved the bodies buried there in a mummified state, with few signs of decomposition. If you want to see the reason Bram Stoker lurked here, visitors are welcome (tours Monday to Friday 9:45 A.M.–12:45 P.M. and 2:00 P.M.–4:45 P.M., Saturday 10:00 A.M.–12:45 P.M.; entrance fee: adults IR£1.20, children 50p, group rates and concessions). Afterwards, you may well need to drop in at the **Irish Whiskey Corner** (see page 63) in cobbled Bow Street.

Parnell Square

Church Street leads into Constitution Hill (from which you will have a fine view of the mountains). To the right are the house and small grounds of the **King's Inns**, yet another James Gandon masterpiece, and also his last — the building was eventually completed by others. The grounds are open to the general public.

Stroll down the streets of this once-fashionable area for a look at the houses, particularly **Parnell Square**, which is also the site of many interesting galleries and museums. In 1801 the Act of Union put a stop to speculative building in this part of the city. The **Garden of Remembrance** on the north side of Parnell Square is a peaceful place to rest. It is dedicated to those who lost their lives in the cause of Irish freedom and features a cruciform lake and the beautiful Oisín Kelly *Children of Lir* (his powerful monument to Jim Larkin can be seen in O'Connell Street; see page 38).

Across the road from the Garden of Remembrance are the **Hugh Lane Municipal Gallery of Modern Art** (see page 62) and the **Dublin Writers Museum** (see page 60). The gallery is set in the 18th-century Charlemont House, built for Lord Charlemont by Sir William Chambers. Restored in 1991, this beautiful building is worth seeing for itself alone, as well as for the splendid art collection. The museum next door (also restored in 1991) is an intriguing combination of Georgian exterior with Victorian interior. Both the museum and gallery have good cafés and restaurants.

East of Parnell Square, in Great George's Street, is the **James Joyce Cultural Centre** (see page 64), housed in a mansion dating from 1784 and run by Joyce's nephew. (Open with a full programme of events, including lectures.)

Children may wish to see the **National Wax Museum** in Granby Row, which includes a Chamber of Horrors, scenes from fairy tale and fantasy, a Hall of the Megastars (devoted to pop musicians), Da Vinci's Last Supper and four popes! (Monday to Saturday 10:00 A.M.–6:00 P.M., Sunday noon–6:00 P.M.)

On the south side of Parnell Square are the **Rotunda** and the **Gate Theatre** (see page 89). The Palladian-style Rotunda contains the oldest maternity hospital in the British Isles and was built in 1751-1755. The chapel itself was constructed 15 years later and has had

The beautiful interiors of the Dublin Writers Museum count among its delightful attractions.

a varied career as an Assembly Room and a cinema (its present function); Charles Dickens also gave readings here. The baroque interior has internationally famed plasterwork.

What is now the Gate Theatre was built in 1784 and is probably the most beautiful stage in Dublin. The theatre company was founded in 1930 by Michael MacLiammoir and Hilton Edwards, and is still going strong today, with an excellent reputation for innovative work, dedicated to serious drama from all over the world. James Mason and Orson Welles began their acting careers here.

O'Connell Street

South of Parnell Square is Upper O'Connell Street. **O'Connell Street** is in fact a grand, wide boulevard, studded with monuments and statues. It runs in a straight line to O'Connell Bridge over the Liffey, and the best way to view it is to

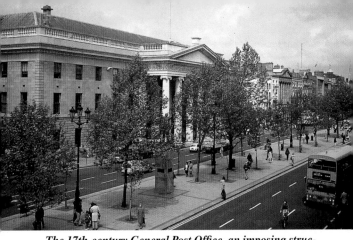

The 17th-century General Post Office, an imposing structure that was fully restored after its devastation in 1916.

walk down the central islands, making excursions to left and right using the zebra crossings.

The road was largely obliterated in the destruction of the Rising (see page 18), but was restored by the end of the 1920s. At the northern end is the 1911 monument to **Parnell** by Augustus Saint-Gaudens. Notice anything odd? Yes, he is wearing two overcoats (apparently he always did).

Statues and monuments of note in O'Connell Street also include the memorial to working-class hero, orator, and socialist **Jim Larkin** by Oisín Kelly (opposite the famous chiming clock of **Clerys**, the largest department store in Ireland); the **Anna Livia Fountain** (the so-called "Floozie in the Jacuzzi") unveiled in 1988 as part of Dublin's millennial celebrations; and John Henry Foley's statue of the Catholic leader **Daniel O'Connell** (if you look carefully, you'll see bullet marks from 1922).

Farther down from the Parnell monument on the left is the north's equivalent of the Shelbourne, the **Gresham Hotel** (built in 1817, seven years before the Shelbourne, it just takes precedence). The Georgian interior of the ground floor is worth a look.

Perhaps the greatest "monument" in Dublin, with pride of place in the centre of O'Connell Street, is the imposingly large **General Post Office**. Built in 1815-1818 and one of the last great buildings of Dublin Georgian architecture, the GPO is justly renowned for its imposing Ionic portico with six fluted columns and its three figures of *Fidelity, Hibernia,* and *Mercury* (sculpted by Edward Smyth, also responsible for most of the carving on the Custom House). It seems almost sacrilegious to buy your postcards in this building but do, because it was here in 1916 — just after the building had been redecorated — that James Connolly and Patrick Pearse proclaimed the Republic after barricading themselves in. The post office was virtually destroyed in the fighting but has since been fully restored. The Rising is commemorated in the main hall by an imposing bronze statue of the mythic folk hero Cuchulainn. The Irish GPO tricolour flies proudly on the roof.

Opposite the Post Office, just into **Earl Street**, is a rather jaunty street-level statue of the ubiquitous James Joyce. Just off from Lower O'Connell Street in Lower Abbey Street is the **Abbey Theatre** (see page 89). Founded in 1904 by W.B. Yeats, Lady Augusta Gregory, and Edward Martyn, the theatre has been a showcase for great Irish writing, including the works of Friel, Leonard, Roche, O'Casey, and Synge (the latter two provoked riots in the audience). Unfortunately, the present Abbey Theatre dates only from 1966, since a fire in 1951 destroyed the original building.

North of the Abbey Theatre and parallel with O'Connell Street in Marlborough Street is the Catholic **St. Mary's**

Pro-Cathedral, the main Catholic parish church of the city cen-tre (St. Patrick's and Christ Church are both Protestant Church of Ireland; see page 15). It is difficult to be entirely pleased with its architecture, which seems to dwarf the street (it was designed originally for O'Connell Street). Built in 1816-1825, it has a somewhat forbidding classical Doric exterior, while the domed Renaissance interior is in restrained blues and greys, and is curiously unadorned for a Catholic Cathedral. However, the spooky crypt is worth a visit, and the Palestrina choir that sings mass on Sundays is excellent, which accounts for the number of visitors.

Still in Marlborough Street and opposite the cathedral is **Ty-rone House** (not open to the public), home to the Department of Education. Built in 1742 by Richard Castle, the interior features work by the Francini brothers (who were also responsible for Newman House; see page 32). Outside is a gift to the people of Ireland from the Italian government in gratitude for relief supplies during World War II: a marble *Pieta* entitled *La Deposizione,* by Ermenegildo Luppi.

You can't miss the Wellington Monument in Phoenix Park, but there's plenty more to see.

Walking back down Marlborough Street, the 16-storey Liberty Hall comes into view again. Built in the 1960s and home to the Transport and General Workers Union, this skyscraper can be seen looming all over the city and has continued to generate criticism. The roof of the Irish

Life Centre, which juts above the skyline behind the Custom House, is another eyesore, although it is partially redeemed by Oisín Kelly's *Chariot of Life* fountain.

The **Irish Life Exhibition Centre** at the left of the shopping mall, is where temporary exhibitions of new Irish arts and crafts are held, and it is also the venue for the annual exhibition of the Craft Potters Society of Ireland.

Similarly controversial is the green glass and stone of the **International Financial Services Centre** in the Custom House Docks redevelopment.

It is as well to finish on a high note, though, and the **Custom House** unequivocally provides it. Built in 1791 and designed by James Gandon as his first Dublin masterpiece, it has undergone thorough renovation (in 1921 it was on fire for five days) and can perhaps be best appreciated from the south bank of the river, though more detail can be seen from the closer vantage point on the north bank.

The elegance and grace of this building have something to do with its human dimensions, for although it stands at 114 meters (375 feet) high and 61 meters (200 feet) wide, its height does not in the least overwhelm. The sculpture on the dome (a personification of Commerce) and the river gods (including Anna Livia, set over the main door) are by Edward Smyth, who was also responsible for the statues on the GPO (see page 39). The original wax models of the river gods are on display in the Civic Museum. The north side of the building has statues by Joseph Banks depicting Africa, America, Asia, and Europe.

PHOENIX PARK

On the banks of the Liffey, just 3 km (2 miles) from the bustle of O'Connell Street, lies the biggest urban park in Europe, comprising some 709 hectares (1,750 acres) of landscaped gardens, woods, pastures, and playing fields. All sorts of sports are played here, and the park incorporates a 9 hectare (22-acre) people's flower garden started in 1864 and a 1735 magazine fort. Phoenix Park is a graceful and elegant expanse with fine views of the mountains, much loved by Dubliners since it was first opened to the public in 1747. Self-guided heritage walks and several nature trails are marked by black information plaques, and herds of deer roam through the grounds.

The oldest building in the park is **Ashtown Castle**, a former papal residence which has been renovated to house a most splendid visitor centre (open 9:30 A.M.–6:30 P.M.; entrance fee: adults IR£2, children IR£1; concessions; disabled access), which presents a video and an excellent two-floor exhibition on the history and wildlife of the park. The exhibition area contains eight superb handcrafted rope wallhangings.

The castle itself (open daily 9:30 A.M.–6:30 P.M. June to September; earlier closing rest of year) comprises an early 17th-century tower house, restored with Irish oak from the park which is held together without a single nail. Outside there is a young garden maze, marking the outline of the original foundations, and a restful café.

The park also boasts the largest obelisk in Europe (and possibly the world) in the 67 meters (220 foot) high **Wellington Monument**, erected in 1861 after the victory of Waterloo. The Wicklow granite is faced with plaques cast from captured and melted-down cannon. Not quite as large is the impressive **Papal Cross**, commemorating Pope John Paul II's visit in 1979, when more than one million people gathered to celebrate mass.

The Phoenix Column, dating from 1747, stands tall near the natural spring from which the name of the park is derived (the result of an English corruption of the Gaelic *fionn uisce*, meaning "clear water").

Occupying more than 12 hectares (30 acres), **Dublin Zoo** (open Monday to Saturday 9:30 A.M.–6:00 P.M., Sunday 10:00 A.M.–6:00 P.M.; entrance fee: adults IR£5.50, children IR£2.90, under three free; family tickets and concessions) is one of the largest in Europe and was founded in 1831. The landscaped grounds (designed by Decimus Burton, who was also responsible for the park lodges) provide a safe home to many endangered species,

In Dublin's Bohemian quarter, pubs and cafés are inclined to spill onto the streets.

including lions, and young children will love the Pet's Corner and zoo train.

Also within the grounds of the park are the official residence of the president of the Republic, which dates from 1751 (not open to the general public) and the U.S. ambassador's residence, an 18th-century house which was formerly the official residence of the Viceroy's chief secretary.

OLD DUBLIN

Temple Bar

To the west of Grafton Street, between the river and Dame Street, is the area of **Temple Bar**, Dublin's Bohemian quarter and an interesting place to explore (there is an information centre at 18 Eustace Street). Here you will find narrow cobbled lanes dating from the 18th century, and still mercifully

Dublin Castle is an archtectural and cultural symbol, established over many centuries.

free of traffic, some charming architecture, and many lively cafés and restaurants (it's one of the best areas to find something to eat in Dublin, particularly ethnic foods).

Temple Bar is home to a wealth of artists and musicians of all styles and degrees of talent. The commercial life of the area reflects this population, with crafts and art workshops, galleries, secondhand clothes and music shops. It also has a very good nightlife, with bars, cinemas, nightclubs, and a variety of theatres.

Everywhere you go you'll see lots of renewal projects. The **Irish Film Centre** (see page 62) in Eustace Street is an imaginative development of an old Friends Meeting House, with a thoroughly recommendable café. You'll notice some street art in Temple Bar: sculpture and installations appear and disappear in the most unlikely places as part of a continuing artistic programme. So just soak up the atmosphere and enjoy.

This area is targeted to become the glittering centre of the city's artistic and cultural life, with a Photography Centre, Gallery and Studio complex, Print Studios, Viking Museum,

Craft Centre and Children's Cultural Centre, as well as a Music Centre and Multi-Media Centre. Find out more at the information centre in Eustace Street.

Leaving Temple Bar from the west, you will discover a long succession of some of the finest buildings in the city. The **Olympia Theatre** (see page 89) at the west end of Dame Street completes a road of remarkable Victorian civic architecture. Built in 1870, its canopy of stained glass and cast iron is the oldest and best in Dublin. Its enthusiastic interior decoration is also typical of the era. Happily, the restored theatre leads a bustling, active life, putting on a regular schedule of plays and concerts. Grab the opportunity to take a good look inside.

Just across the way is Dublin's **City Hall** (open Monday-Friday 10:00 A.M.–1:00 P.M. and 2:15–5:00 P.M.), home to the Dublin Corporation but built originally as the Royal Exchange in 1779. This fine building, with its Corinthian portico facing Parliament Street and the river, is suitably impressive for a former centre of commerce, and the interior is even more interesting. The columned rotunda is graced with a breathtaking mosaic dome, and there are sculptures by Edward Smyth and some superb carving by Simon Vierpyl.

The building was designed by Thomas Cooley and stands on the site of the Former Lucas Coffee House and Eagle Tavern, whose customers — a group of young Dublin blades — went on to found the Hell Fire Club in 1735. City Hall was also the scene of Parnell's funeral.

Dublin Castle

The City Hall leads the visitor naturally to **Dublin Castle** (Monday-Friday for half-hour guided tours, 10:00 A.M.–12:15 P.M., 2:00–5:00 P.M.; and Saturday-Sunday 2:00–5:00 P.M., entrance fee: IR£1.75), by virtue of its age one of the most architecturally complex buildings in the city and a monument full of symbolic resonance for all Dubliners.

Walking through the imposing Great Gate to the beautiful Georgian "yard," it is difficult to see why the building was once so feared as a place of punishment, torture, and death, for it was the centre of British military and social power over the city, and used as a prison. Since 1922, however, it has been the scene of various ceremonial events (including the inauguration of Irish presidents) and the location for EU summit meetings.

The castle comprises a series of architectural layers, the oldest of which is shown in the **Viking and Norman Defences Exhibition**, a small but exciting underground display of defences uncovered during restoration work in 1986. Here visitors can stand in the dry bed of the old moat, and there are gangways imaginatively lit over the waters of the encroaching river seeking its old course (children will love this).

The guided tour commences with the **State Apartments**, which is probably the highlight of any visit. Much of the furniture is original to the castle. Keep your eyes on the ceilings and floors: there are some beautiful ceilings from other houses and equally splendid Irish carpets. The **Wedgewood Room** is the former billiard room and contains a Phoenix carpet given by De Valera, while in the **Drawing Room** a Ming punch bowl provides the tones for the turquoise Louis Quinze chairs. Notice, too, the many petticoat mirrors around the room, in which the ladies could check discreetly the state of their skirts. The **Connolly Room** is so called because it was here that the wounded James Connolly spent his last night before being executed, while the lovely **Portrait Gallery** contains convex wall mirrors so the host at table could keep his eye on everyone, particularly the servants.

A magnificent carpet, the design of which is based on a page from the Book of Kells (see page 68), covers the floor of the **Throne Room** (the throne was last used in 1911 by George V).

The enormous **St. Patrick's Hall** has a frieze depicting the arms of the Knights of St. Patrick, and on the top landing, you'll see a carpet showing the *Children of Lir* (an old Irish myth, in which the children are changed into swans by their stepmother). In the restored **Treasury** (built in 1715 and located in the Lower Yard), browse in the bookshop or relax in the **Castle Vaults Bistro and Patisserie**, which makes for pleasant and cheap self-service dining, inside and out.

Formerly the Chapel Royal, the Gothic-revival **Church of the Holy Trinity** was built in 1807-1814, and is delightfully furnished with detailed stone and wood carving featuring coats of arms on the gallery (much of the stone work is by Smyth), stucco work, and a fan-vaulted ceiling. Beneath, in the vaults, is a small exhibition space. The **Castle Hall**, opposite the State Apartments, holds exhibitions from State collections; its combination of dark wood and light stone is visually refreshing.

Outside, much of the medieval towers remain to be seen, and you can walk through the Cork Tower to the delightful modern roof gardens.

Christ Church Cathedral, to which St. Lawrence O'Toole quite literally lost his heart.

Christ Church Cathedral

Left down Castle Street from the Great Gate is the first of the two cathedrals in the area, **Christ Church Cathedral** in Christchurch Place. Stand-

ing, like the castle, on an eminence, the cathedral rises on the site of King Sitric's wooden church built in 1038, and in parts is the oldest building in Dublin, dating back to the 1170s.

The cathedral was rebuilt in the 1170s at the instigation of "Strongbow," Earl of Pembroke, whose tomb lies inside. In 1487, it was the scene of the coronation of the pretender to the throne, Lambert Simnel. Unfortunately, the building was massively and largely unsympathetically restored in 1871-1878, when much of the interior was ripped out.

However, there is still much to appreciate in Christ Church, including the impressive stonework in the nave, the handsome 19th-century floor tiles based on a 13th-century pattern, and the large vaulted crypt (used as a tavern in medieval times) with intriguing displays that include the skeletons of a cat and a rat found in the organ pipes and a set of stocks dating from 1670. (You could easily imagine Bram Stoker prowling around here as well.) Perhaps even more macabre is the embalmed heart of St. Lawrence O'Toole (a 12th-century Archbishop of Dublin), which is kept in a cage suspended on the wall near the altar, in the **Chapel of St. Loo**.

In **Fishamble Street**, nearby, a black plaque commemorates the first performance of Handel's *Messiah*, which took place in the Music Hall (now an old steelworks) on 13 April 1742. In the old Synod Hall just across the road from the cathedral (but linked to it by a delicate bridge) you will find **Dublinia**, a realistic sight-and-sound re-creation, in five languages, of Dublin in medieval times, complete with sounds and smells, a medieval maze, and craftsmen at work. Dublinia covers the growth of the city from the Anglo-Norman invasion (1170) to the dissolution of the monasteries in 1540. (Open April to September daily 10:00 A.M.–5:00 P.M., October to March 11:00 A.M.–4:00 P.M. [4:30 P.M. Sundays]; entrance fee: adults IR£3.95, children IR£2.90, ask about concessions.) The beautifully restored three-storey hall was first built in the 1870s.

Wood Quay, on the south bank of the river on the other side of the cathedral (downhill from the arch), is dominated by the brutalist offices of the Dublin Corporation, and is the site of the original Viking settlement. Construction of the offices, however, obliterated much of the archaeological dig which had unearthed the original layout of the 9th-century quay, but the Viking artifacts found here are on view in the National Museum (see page 65) and in Dublinia. It is hoped that eventually the Wood Quay dig will be incorporated into the redevelopment plans of Temple Bar (see page 43).

The remaining parts of the dig, which will go on for some years, are visible from the top deck of a passing double-decker bus! On the sidewalks of Wood Quay, Fishamble Street, Winetavern Street, and Christchurch Place, your attention will be drawn to the work of Rachel Joynt, a series of 18 designs in bronze, steel, and granite reflecting the artifacts found there and the trades and crafts they represent. *Woodkey Walk*, as it is known, was produced in 1992; an explanatory leaflet is available from Dublin Tourism.

In **High Street** are the two **St. Audoen's Churches**. The restored Church of Ireland St. Audoen's is the older of the two churches (c. 1190) and is, indeed, the only truly medieval church in the city. The impressive neoclassical Catholic St. Audoen's was built in 1847 and has an audio-visual exhibition of its own (*The Flame on the Hill*) about pre-Viking Ireland. Both churches stand beside what remains of the old city walls, and St. Audoen's is the only surviving gate (the High Street itself was a medieval road on which stood the High Cross of the Norman city, where decrees and notices of excommunication were read out). Elsewhere, granite markers erected in 1991 indicate the line of the old city walls.

West from here in **Thomas Street**, a plaque on the decommissioned and rather sad **St. Catherine's Church** (built in 1769) marks the spot where famed Irish resistance hero Robert Emmet was hanged in 1803 (see page 17).

Thomas Street West turns into **James's Street**, where the **Guinness Brewery** has been situated since 1759, and nearby in Crane Street is the **Guinness Hop Store** (see page 61) and **Visitor Centre** (open Monday-Friday 10:00 A.M.–4:30 P.M., entrance fee: IR£2), the latter housing the World of Guinness Exhibition, an audio-visual display (last show at 3:30 P.M.), museum, and bar with free samples!

The Liberties

These streets (marked by the junction at the west end of **Upper Kevin Street**) are situated in an area known as the Liberties (because it stretched outside the medieval city walls and consequently enjoyed a certain degree of freedom and autonomy). In **Back Lane**, between Francis Street and

Facing Mother Redcap's Market, Tailors' Hall dates back to the early 18th century.

the two St. Audoen's, you will find **Mother Redcap's Market**. Molly Malone may or may not have been here, but it is certainly worth coming to this large covered market for the books, antiques, and crafts, and some of the food stalls selling fresh Irish produce are extremely difficult to resist.

Also in Back Lane (through the arch opposite the market) are the headquarters of *An Taisce*, an organization dedicated to the preservation and upkeep of historic buildings and gardens. Appropriately for such an organization, its home is the delightful **Tailors' Hall** which, dating from 1706, is the oldest guild hall in Ireland and one of the few remaining original Queen Anne buildings in Dublin. In addition to the tailors, hosiers, and barber-surgeons made use of the hall.

St. Patrick's Cathedral

At the eastern end of Back Lane and turning right, Nicholas Street becomes Patrick Street, and in St. Patrick's close is the cathedral. St. Patrick's (entrance IR£1) holds a number of records: St. Patrick himself is reputed to have baptized converts on this spot (marked by a Celtic cross in the nave), indicating that there has been a church here since around A.D. 450, making it the oldest Christian site in Dublin; the 43-meter (141-foot) tower holds the largest ringing peal of bells in Ireland; and the 90-meter (300-foot) interior makes it the longest church in the country.

The height and space of the cathedral are impressive, particularly the transepts, behind which is an ornate spiral staircase. Note the carved helmets and swords set above the choir stalls and the 19th-century tiled floor. Not much is left of the original construction of 1191: destroyed in a fire in the 14th century, it was later rebuilt, and even included some Victorian restoration work, though not as extensive as that in Christ Church (see page 47).

The cathedral has had a varied and interesting history, and enjoys a lively rivalry with Christ Church, only a few hundred yards away (St. Patrick's is the national cathedral of the Church of Ireland). From 1320 until its closure by Henry VIII, it was the seat of the first university in Ireland before Trinity was founded. Cromwellian troops stabled their horses in the aisles; the great Jonathan Swift was dean here from 1713-1745 (his grave lies in the cathedral, as does that of his great love, Esther Johnson). You can also see the pulpit from which he preached.

An interesting feature from the medieval **Chapter House** is a door with a hole in it. The hole was cut in 1492 by Lord Kildare so he could reassure his archenemy Lord Ormonde, who was under siege in the Chapter House, of his friendly intentions. Kildare put his arm through the hole, thus giving rise to the common expression "to chance your arm."

Within the surrounding 19th-century **St. Patrick's Park**, the site of St. Patrick's well is marked, and there are memorials to famous Dublin writers.

Also in the close (left out of the cathedral exit) is **Marsh's Library** (open Monday and Wednesday through Friday from 10:00 A.M.–12:45 P.M. and 2:00 P.M.–5:00 P.M.; and Saturday 10:30 A.M.–12:45 P.M.; free, but a voluntary contribution is most appreciated; ring the bell for entrance). Home to more than 25,000 books, the L-shaped library was founded in 1701 by Archbishop Narcissus Marsh and was the first public library in Ireland.

Venerable tomes line the oak shelves of Marsh's Library, established in 1701.

The scholarly tomes are for the most part works of theology, medicine, and ancient languages. The oak shelving is original, as are the metal cages in which scholars were locked so as to prevent thefts. The on-premises bindery repairs and restores old books and manuscripts. Even if you aren't a scholar, do come here — for the atmosphere and beauty of the place is entrancing.

Door-spotting at its best in Merrion Square, where each Georgian entranceway has its own design.

GEORGIAN DUBLIN

So much of the rich history and architecture of Dublin stems from the Georgian era that it may appear rather arbitrary to designate one area of the city as "Georgian." However, the architectural harmonies of the streets and squares lying to the southeast of Nassau Street offer the visitor so much of interest and make for such delightful walking that, of all areas of the city, this is the one that truly deserves to be called "Georgian." In addition to the superb buildings, there are several important museums and galleries to visit, and the banks of the Grand Canal provide leafy, shaded walks.

Merrion Square

Clare Street, at the eastern end of Nassau Street, in turn runs into **Merrion Square North**, dating from 1762 and containing some of the finest houses in the square. The houses here were the homes of high society, including many members of parliament and famous artists and writers. Look for the little individual details on the houses — variations in the designs of the doors and fanlights, and the different kinds of knockers, some in the form of a fish or a human hand.

Number 8 belongs to Ireland's **Royal Institute of Architects**; it's open to the public (see page 67), while at no. 73 on the south side of the square is the **Irish Architectural Archive** (see page 62), a library of architectural materials which is also open to the public.

In Merrion Square West is the **National Gallery of Ireland** (see page 64), which has a self-service restaurant and will also provide tickets for the free Saturday tours of the restored Edwardian baroque **Government Buildings** in Upper Merrion

---

Sons and Daughters

Dublin has produced some famous artists and writers, politicians and intellectuals in its long history, and many of the houses associated with them have commemorative plaques, particularly those around Merrion Square (DANIEL O'CONNELL lived at number 58, for example). Novelist ELIZABETH BOWEN was born at 15 Herbert Place, off Baggot Street, while philosopher EDMUND BURKE started life at 17 Arran Quay. JAMES JOYCE was born at 41 Brighton Square, Rathgar, but lived at a total of 23 Dublin addresses, including 14 Fitzgibbon Street, 29 Hardwicke Street, and 17 North Richmond Street.

Playwright GEORGE BERNARD SHAW was born at 33 Synge Street, and fellow dramatist and parliamentarian RICHARD BRINSLEY SHERIDAN at 12 Dorset Street. JONATHAN SWIFT was born at 7 Hoey's Court, and the DUKE OF WELLINGTON at Mornington House, 24 Upper Merrion Street. OSCAR WILDE lived at 15 Westland Row and 1 Merrion Square, while W.B. YEATS, poet and co-founder of the Abbey Theatre, was born at 5 Sandymount Avenue and lived at 52 *and* 82 Merrion Square. ERWIN SCHRODINGER, who won the Physics Nobel Prize for his work on wave mechanics, worked at 65 Merrion Square.

Street (open Saturday from 10:30 A.M.–12:45 P.M., and from 1:30–4:45 P.M.; no pre-booking required). Refurbished in 1990-1991 and housing the offices and meeting rooms of the *Taoiseach* (prime minister) and his cabinet, the interior rooms of the Government Buildings are a fascinating and tasteful combination of the old and the new. Together with the latest technology, the prime minister's office has a superb Bossi marble fireplace, as well as a fine display of art and crafts.

A magnificent Evie Hone stained-glass window adorns the landing in the main entrance; it is beautifully comple- mented by the carpet and balustrade designed by Mary Fitzgerald. There is some excellent contemporary furniture made from traditional materials and a miniature of Oisín Kel- ly's sculpture *The Children of Lir*. Outside, the courtyard, paved in limestone tram-setts from the streets of Old Dublin, is graced with a water fountain.

In Merrion Street stands the imposing Victorian building of the **Natural History Museum** (see page 66), nicknamed "The Dead Zoo" by locals.

Walk through to **Merrion Square Park**, entering one of the many gates, and walk along some of the secret paths and the immaculately groomed gardens to discover why, like St. Stephen's, it is such a magnet for people at lunchtime. You'll want to return here, particularly as the "**Boulevard Galleries**" (see page 58) set up around the square weekends. It wasn't always so pleasant, however: at the height of the Great Famine in 1845-1847, a soup kitchen was set up and run from here to help starving refugees.

Fitzwilliam Square and Ballsbridge

Take time to stroll down the streets around Merrion Square, which date from the same era and many of which were laid out at the same time as the square. At the eastern end of Upper

Mount Street you'll notice the distinctive shape of the Greek-revival **St. Stephen's Church**, which dates back to 1824. For obvious reasons it is known universally as the Peppercanister Church; occasional events and concerts are held here. **Lower Fitzwilliam Street**, at the southeast corner of Merrion Square, houses the offices of the Electricity Supply Board. They made up for the ugliness of their new building by restoring **29 Lower Fitzwilliam Street**, a museum house open to the public (see page 66).

The street crosses Lower Baggot Street and leads on to **Fitzwilliam Square**, another fine place with a park open to residents only. The last of Dublin's Georgian squares to be built, it was completed by 1830, although the older houses date back to 1714. Here, as elsewhere in Georgian Dublin, note the little variations in detail in the doorways and fanlights, and in the ironwork of the balconies and bootscrapers as well as doorknockers.

For a peaceful perspective on the city, stroll along the towpath of the Grand Canal.

Back in Baggot Street is the office of the **Bank of Ireland**. The bank's Arts Centre, showing part of the collection of modern Irish art, can be found at the back of the College Green branch (see page 28). The road was named after Baggotrath Castle, which stood here until the early 19th century. At **Baggot Street Bridge** you can drop in at the information centre at the headquarters of the **Irish Tourist Board**, and farther along the towpath you can chat to **Patrick Kavanagh**, sitting on a bench: actually, it's a life-sized bronze commemorating the Irish poet, who died in 1967.

The **Grand Canal**, begun in 1755, has a pleasant towpath walk under a canopy of leaves, past the gardens of terraced houses and behind offices and mansions. There are plenty of ducks, moorhens, and swans and the canal is spanned by the very distinctive curves of many 18th-century bridges. This is a good place to rest and recuperate, and gain a different slant on life in the city: stroll between Baggot Street Bridge and Leeson Street Bridge, or in the opposite direction toward Huband Bridge.

Beyond Baggot Street Bridge to the east is the suburb of **Ballsbridge**, at the heart of which are the grounds of the **Royal Dublin Society**. The society was founded in 1731, and established among other things the National Gallery and the National Library. All sorts of events and concerts are held at the showground, however, including the Spring Show and Garden Festival and the Dublin Horse Show.

On the corner of Elgin and Pembroke Road is the **American Embassy**, conceived by an American and Irish architect in 1964, and beyond it in Shrewsbury Road, the **Chester Beatty Library and Gallery of Oriental Art** (soon to relocate to Dublin Castle) (see page 58). A mining engineer from Colorado, Sir Alfred Chester Beatty, bequeathed this collection to the Irish nation in 1956.

MUSEUMS AND GALLERIES

Dublin has so many museums and galleries that it is virtually impossible to list them all. Here, we are covering the most important and interesting ones. Most are closed on Monday

— some also close on Sunday — and opening hours tend to be restricted during the winter months.

A "Passport to Dublin's Heritage" ticket, available at any Dublin Tourist Information Office or participating attraction, saves both time and money and includes entry to the Dublin Writers Museum, Guinness Hop Store, Irish Museum of Modern Art, National Museum of Ireland, and Trinity College. Details of all current prices can be found in *The Inside Guide to Dublin* booklet provided by tourist information centres; a variety of leaflets is also available at many galleries and museums.

For a quick reference guide, see our list of Museum Highlights, on the opposite page.

"Boulevard Galleries"
Merrion Square and St. Stephen's Green.
Every Saturday and Sunday in summer the railings around these squares are transformed into giant outdoor art galleries, as hundreds of artists display their work. It's great fun to browse and buy.

Chester Beatty Library and Gallery of Oriental Art
20 Shrewsbury Road, Ballsbridge, Dublin 4. DART: Sandymount Street.
A treasure house of manuscripts and paintings, books and furniture from Western and Eastern cultures. The actual Chester Beatty Library includes copies of the Koran and codices dating from the 2nd century B.C. Guided tours take place on Wednesday and Saturday at 2:30 P.M. There is also a library for scholars and a bookshop. Tuesday–Friday 10:00 A.M.–5:00 P.M., Saturday 2:00–5:00 P.M.; closed Sunday, Monday, and Tuesday after Bank Holiday Monday; free.

City Arts Centre
23 Moss Street, Dublin 2.
Situated in an attractive site on the south bank of the Liffey,

MUSEUM HIGHLIGHTS

Dublin Writers Museum: *18/19 Parnell Square North, Dublin 1.* Devoted to the life and work of great Irish writers and the history of Irish literature; very popular. Monday–Saturday 10am-5pm, Sunday 11:30-6pm; IR£2.90, children IR£1.20. Passes available to include Shaw House, Joyce Tower. (See page 60.)

Hugh Lane Municipal Gallery of Modern Art: *Charlemont House, Parnell Square North, Dublin 1.* Famous 20th-century art, including works by Courbet, Manet, Monet, and various Irish artists. Tuesday-Friday 9:30am-6pm, Saturday 9:30am-5pm, Sunday 11am-5pm; closed Monday; free. (See page 62.)

Irish Museum of Modern Art: *Royal Hospital, Military Road, Kilmainham, Dublin 8.* A permanent collection of Irish and international art mainly from the second half of the 20th century, complemented by changing exhibitions. Tuesday-Saturday 10am-5:30pm, Sunday noon-5:30pm; closed Monday; guided tours Wednesday and Friday 2:30pm, Saturday 11:30am; free. (See page 63.)

Kilmainham Gaol: *Inchicore Road, Kilmainham, Dublin 8.* A prison for 130 years and dating back to 1795, where leaders of many rebellions were imprisoned, including Emmet and Parnell. Audio-visual and a guided tour. Daily 10am-6pm, May-September, shorter hours in winter; IR£2, children IR£1. (See page 64.)

National Gallery of Ireland: *Merrion Square West, Dublin 2.* Opened in 1864, and now a vast collection, with every major school represented. Monday-Saturday 10am-5:30pm (Thursday 10am-8.:30pm), Sunday 2-5pm; free. (See page 64.)

National Museum of Ireland: *Kildare Street, Dublin 2.* Everything from Viking artifacts to prehistoric and medieval jewellery, and a display devoted to the 1916 Rising and War of Independence. Tuesday-Saturday 10am-5pm, Sunday 2-5pm; closed Monday; free. Guided tours daily 10:30am, 11:30am, 1pm, 2:15pm, 3:30pm, Sundays 2:15pm, 3:15pm, 4pm; IR£1. (See page 65.)

Number 29: *29 Lower Fitzwilliam Street, Dublin 2.* A restored Georgian townhouse, typically furnished to reflect middle-class life around 1790-1820. Many paintings and furnishings are on loan from the National Museum, and there is a charming collection of dolls and toys in the nursery. Audio-visual and guided tour (10 people maximum). Tuesday-Saturday 10am-5pm, Sunday 2-5pm; closed Monday; free. (See page 66.)

right opposite the new Custom House Development, this new complex of galleries, exhibition areas and theatre space caters to local groups and artists and, as you would expect from a venture backed by rock group U2, is geared to younger adults. There is disabled access and an excellent café with a fine view of the Custom House. Open daily 9:30 A.M.–10:00 P.M., galleries open 11:00 A.M.

Civic Museum
58 South William Street, Dublin 2.
This small, quirky museum offers a sidelong glance at the history of Dublin through its collections of prints and other ephemera. With an emphasis on the hidden life of the city, you'll come across such things as old street signs and wooden water mains, coal-hole covers and the original wax models of the river gods on the Custom House, and the lesser-known people who shaped the life of Dublin. A satellite photograph of the city hangs on the stairs. Tuesday–Saturday 10:00 A.M.–6:00 P.M., Sunday 11:00 A.M.–2:00 P.M.; closed Monday; free.

Douglas Hyde Gallery
Trinity College, Nassau Street entrance, Dublin 2.
The place to go in Dublin for the contemporary and avant-garde in Irish and international art. The modern building has a two-storey exhibition space and hosts all sorts of events and performances. Monday–Friday 11:00 A.M.–6:00 P.M. (Thursday 7:00 P.M.), Saturday 11:00 A.M.–4:45 P.M.; lectures Wednesday 1:15 P.M., tours noon Saturday; free.

Dublin Writers Museum
18/19 Parnell Square North, Dublin 1.
It's a real pleasure to wander through this light and elegant museum, with chandeliers illuminating the charming plaster ceilings. As you would expect, novelists and playwrights with Dublin connections, from Jonathan Swift to Brendan Behan, are well represented. As well as collections of rare

editions, manuscripts, and memorabilia, there is a portrait gallery, a bookshop, café, and restaurant.

There are frequent exhibitions and events, and the Writers Centre provides a place for talk and work. There is even a Zen garden. Monday-Saturday 10:00 A.M.–5:00 P.M., and Sunday 11:30 A.M.–6:00 P.M.; June–August: Monday–Friday 10:00 A.M.–7:00 P.M.; audio tours and pamphlets available in various languages; entrance IR£2.90, children IR£1.20; combined ticket for Shaw House, James Joyce Tower, Sandycove, and Dublin Writers Museum IR£6.30, children IR£2.130.

Gallery of Photography
Meeting House Square, Sycamore Street, Temple Bar.
Photographs of Dublin past and present in the city's only gallery of photography. Exhibitions are held of Irish and international photography, and there are also books and posters for sale. Open 11:00 A.M.–6:00 P.M., Sunday noon–6:00 P.M.; free.

Guinness Hop Store
Crane Street, Dublin 8.
This gallery shares a converted brewery building with the Guinness Visitor Centre and holds a number of exhibitions of contemporary art throughout the year. Paintings and posters are usually the main features. The Visitor Centre (IR£2 entry) presents a wonderful history and evocation of the world of Guinness and is well worth a visit. Store open Monday-Wednesday and Friday 10:00 A.M.–4:30 P.M., Thursday 10:00 A.M.–7:00 P.M.; closed Saturday and Sunday; free.

Heraldic Museum and Genealogical Office
2 Kildare Street, Dublin 2.
As well as the unique history of heraldry (with exhibits that include banners, coins, paintings, and stamps), the consulting service of the office of Ireland's Chief Herald will help you to step back in time when tracing your own ancestry. Open from Monday–Friday 10:00 A.M.–12:30 P.M. and 2:00–4:30 P.M.

Hugh Lane Municipal Gallery of Modern Art

Charlemont House, Parnell Square North, Dublin 1.

Sir Hugh Lane, who died in 1915, bequeathed his collection of paintings to the Irish government and the National Gallery in London. This gallery also includes a variety of work by famous names. The post-impressionist paintings of Jack B. Yeats (brother of the famous poet) are particularly noteworthy (there is also work by modern Irish artists, as well as a fine portrait gallery). There is an excellent café in the basement. Free concerts are held on Sunday lunchtimes from April to June. Open Tuesday–Friday 9:30 A.M.–6:00 P.M., Saturday 9:30 A.M.–5:00 P.M., Sunday 11:00 A.M.–5:00 P.M.; and closed Monday; free; disabled access and toilet facilities.

Irish Architectural Archive

73 Merrion Square, Dublin 2.

This beautiful Georgian house contains archives of drawings, maps, models, photographs and plans of Irish buildings from the 17th century onwards. Tuesday–Friday 10:00 A.M.–1:00 P.M. and 2:30–5:00 P.M.

Irish Film Centre

6 Eustace Street, Temple Bar, Dublin 2.

An exciting and intriguing development in the old Friends Meeting House, this centre now incorporates a National Film Archive, two cinemas, an information centre, a bookshop, and a library. A varied programme of films from around the world is shown throughout the year, and there is also an excellent café. Matinée shows cost IR£2.50, evening shows IR£4; concessions. Weekly membership for IR£1 entitles you to see films with up to three guests.

Irish-Jewish Museum

3/4 Walworth Road, Dublin 8.

The Jewish population of Dublin is smaller now than it once was, but this former synagogue, set in the heart of what was the city's Jewish quarter in the last century, tells the story of the Jews in Ireland by means of documents, various memorabilia, and old photographs (look for a Guinness bottle with a Hebrew label). This is a small museum revealing a little-known part of Dublin's community.

The Shaw Birthplace Museum (see page 67) is only five minutes" walk away, so go on a day when they are both open. Irish-Jewish Museum May–September: Tuesday, Thursday, and Sunday 11:00 A.M. –3:30 P.M.; October–April: Tuesday, Thursday, and Sunday 10:30 A.M.–2:30 P.M. Shaw Birthplace May–October: Monday–Saturday 10:00 A.M.–6:00 P.M.; (Sundays and bank holidays 11:30 A.M.–6:00 P.M.).

Irish Museum of Modern Art

Royal Hospital, Military Road, Kilmainham, Dublin 8.
Like so many of the city's museums, the building housing this one (the restored Royal Hospital) is itself a joy to behold. With wonderful light and space it makes a tremendous exhibition area. The permanent holding includes the Gordon Lambert Collection, presenting over 100 works from the 1960s-1970s. Only parts of the entire collection are exhibited at a time. There are also all sorts of temporary exhibitions and retrospectives, events and concerts, plus a museum bookshop and an unmissable café in the vaults. Good wheelchair access. Open Tuesday–Saturday 10:00 A.M.–5:30 P.M., Sunday noon–5:30 P.M.; closed Monday; some guided tours available Wednesday and Friday 2:30 P.M., Saturday 11:30 A.M.; free.

Irish Whiskey Corner

Irish Distillers, Bow Street, Dublin 7.
This distillery closed in 1972, but the spirit store is the headquarters of Irish Distillers, and next door is the museum. The guided tour and exhibition include a fascinating demonstration of whiskey making and concludes with tastings. Open May–October Monday–Friday tours at 11:00 A.M., 2:30 P.M.,

and 3:30 P.M., or by appointment; Saturday tours at 3:30 P.M.; booking highly recommended.

James Joyce Cultural Centre
35 North Great George's Street, Dublin 1.

A museum in a Georgian mansion built in 1784; the centre contains an archive, museum, and study centre devoted to the great novelist. The building has been completely renovated. Ask at tourist information for opening times.

Kilmainham Gaol
Inchicore Road, Kilmainham, Dublin 8.

This is a powerful and fascinating museum, principally because the internal design of the building is still very much that of a prison. De Valera (see page 19) was the last prisoner (in 1924) and in 1966 he opened the museum, which is dedicated to the memory of the political prisoners the building once held. A 25-minute audio-visual presentation in the prison chapel is followed by a fascinating and sometimes macabre guided tour, and there is also an exhibition and bookshop. Daily 10:00 A.M.–6:00 P.M. (shorter hours in winter); adults IR£2, children IR£1, concessions.

Nearby, on the south bank of the Liffey, is the **Islandbridge Memorial Park**, built in the thirties to designs by Edwin Lutyens (who designed London's Cenotaph). The gardens are a powerful tribute to the thousands of Irish soldiers who died in World War I while serving in the British Army. The sombre design incorporates the *War Stone* and four granite pavilions, one of which contains Celtic and art deco illuminated manuscripts by Harry Clarke (who also designed the windows in Bewley's; see page 23) which list the names of all those killed.

National Gallery of Ireland
Merrion Square West, Dublin 2.

Housed in a beautiful building are works by Brueghel, Constable, El Greco, Fra Angelico, Gainsborough, Goya, Hals, Morisot, Nolde, Picasso, Rembrandt, Ruisdael, and Van Dongen among many others. The collection of Dutch landscapes from the 17th century is particularly noteworthy, as are the startling paintings of Jack B. Yeats. Caravaggio's long-lost *The Taking of Christ* has been on display since 1993, after it was discovered in a Jesuit house in Dublin. Many of the English and Irish paintings depict people and events from Dublin's history. There are also watercolours, drawings, prints, and 300 items of sculpture. With a good bookshop and the excellent Fitzer's café you could easily spend all day here.

On Saturdays only the gallery provides free tickets for same-day guided tours of the Government Buildings in Upper Merrion Street (see page 54). Open all year from Monday to Saturday, 10:00 A.M.–5:30 P.M. (Thursdays until 8:30 P.M.), Sunday 2:00–5:00 P.M.; free.

National Museum of Ireland
Kildare Street, Dublin 2.

Dating back to 1890, this is one of the best museums in Europe, reflecting Ireland's rich history from 2000 B.C. to the present. The Treasury part of the museum houses the gold artifacts and jewellery of prehistoric Ireland right up to the Middle Ages, including the famous Ardagh Chalice, Tara Brooch, and Cross of Cong.

The building has a marvellous domed entrance hall, a mosaic floor, blue and yellow ceramic door surrounds, and intricate ironwork in the central atrium. There is also a good café. Tuesday–Saturday 10:00 A.M.–5:00 P.M., Sunday 2:00–5:00 P.M.; closed Monday; free; guided tours daily 10:30 A.M., 11:30 A.M., 1:00 P.M., 2:15 P.M., 3:30 P.M., Sunday 2:15 P.M., 3:15 P.M., 4:00 P.M.; IR£1.

7-9 Merrion Row houses the Irish Folklife Division and Geological Section of the National Museum of Ireland

(Tuesday–Saturday 10:00 A.M.–5:00 P.M.; closed Monday; free), which hold interesting temporary exhibitions.

Natural History Museum
Merrion Street, Dublin 2.

This is a thorough, comprehensive collection of Ireland's zoology, featuring mammals, birds, fish, butterflies, and insects. There are also collections from around the world.

Everywhere, vast hordes of animals seem to be looking down at you in this packed museum, which makes it a firm favourite with children. Open Tuesday–Saturday 10:00 A.M.–5:00 P.M., Sunday 2:00–5:00 P.M.; closed Monday; free entrance.

Number 29
29 Lower Fitzwilliam Street, Dublin 2.

Number 29 is a lovely Georgian townhouse, typical of the area, which has been restored and superbly fitted out to reflect life in the late 18th to early 19th century, with everything — from carpets to plasterwork, bootscrapers, and bell pulls — either the genuine article or a meticulous reproduction.

An audio-visual display is followed by a half-hour guided tour for a maximum of ten people. The staff are friendly and helpful, and there is a small tearoom. Number 29 can get very busy, so you may have to call back if you don't arrive early. Open Tuesday–Saturday 10:00 A.M.–5:00 P.M., and Sunday from 2:00–5:00 P.M.; closed Monday; free.

Project Arts Centre
39 East Essex Street, Dublin 2.

Sitting right on the cusp of contemporary artistic expression, the Project Arts Centre displays the most avant-garde in painting and sculpture. In addition, it takes on a new dimension when it doubles as a theatre in the evenings. If you want to see what's happening tomorrow, this is definitely the place to come. Open Monday to Saturday from 11:00 A.M.–6:00 P.M.; closed Sunday.

Royal Institute of Architects of Ireland

8 Merrion Square, Dublin 2.

In the appropriately harmonious and aesthetically pleasing surroundings of Merrion Square (see page 53), the Royal Institute of Architects displays a permanent exhibition of the best work of Irish architects, as well as holding frequent temporary exhibitions on all aspects of architecture.

The Institute is open from Monday–Friday 9:30 A.M.–5:00 P.M., closed Saturday and Sunday.

Shaw Birthplace Museum

33 Synge Street, Dublin 8.

The great man's birthplace makes for a fascinating visit in more ways than one. The small Victorian house gives an insight into the lives of a family of more modest means, thus providing an interesting balance to the grander Dublin houses open to the visitor.

An exhibition about Shaw and the Dublin he knew begins in the depths of the basement kitchen, while the small garden

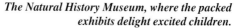

The Natural History Museum, where the packed exhibits delight excited children.

is an attractive place to rest awhile. Tours and booklets are available in a number of languages, and the staff is very friendly. Try to go when the nearby Irish-Jewish Museum (see page 62) is also open.

Open from May–October Monday–Saturday 10:00 A.M.–1:00 P.M., 2:00 – 5:00 P.M., Sunday 11;30 A.M.–6:00 P.M.; adults IR£2.40, children IR£1.10, concessions; a combined ticket is also available for the Dublin Writers Museum, Joyce Tower, at Sandycove, and the Shaw Museum (see page 67), for IR£6.30, children IR£2.30.

Trinity College
College Green, Dublin 2.

The new exhibition area of the Colonnades beneath the Old Library displays the famous Book of Kells, the Book of Durrow, and other beautiful illuminated manuscripts of the Middle Ages. These exquisite artifacts testify to the faith as well as the artistry of unnamed craftsmen who devoted their lives to the work (see page 28).

Different pages of the two well-known treasures are displayed every six weeks, and the entire exhibition is tremendously popular, so be prepared for some long lines at the entrance.

The Dublin Experience, a spectacular audio-visual presentation, gives an introduction to the city with hourly shows 10:00 A.M.–5:00 P.M. daily (also available in French, German and Italian). 9:30 A.M.–5:30 P.M., Sunday noon–5:00 P.M.; Colonnades Gallery IR£2.50, Dublin Experience IR£2.75, Old Library IR£3, combined ticket IR£5.00; half-hour guided tour IR£3.50 (includes the Old Library but not the Dublin Experience).

Waterways Visitor Centre
Grand Canal Basin, Ringsend, off Pearse Street, Dublin 4.

Opened in the summer of 1993, this exciting and imaginative small centre is built on piers over the waters of the canal. With its open observation deck and superb use of glass and the surrounding water, it is rather like being onboard a ship, the perfect architecture for the subject of Ireland's waterways.

An excellent video presents the subject, but the real fun and interest lie in the exhibition, which includes working models and displays devoted to the history and ecology of Ireland's canals. Take time to examine the silk hangings in the main exhibition area. June–September daily 9:30 A.M.–6:30 P.M., restricted times for rest of year; adults IR£2, children IR£1, concessions.

Opposite the centre and set in a restored sugar mill is the **Tower Crafts Design Centre**, which comprises shops, workshops, and a first-floor restaurant. Perfect for a break.

EXCURSIONS

As if the city itself did not provide enough options, the countryside around Dublin offers a wealth of possible excursions and daytrips. The DART railway runs north and south to most seaside towns and villages along the coast, and even operates a guided tour. Perhaps the best place to go on the DART is north to the Howth peninsula, which affords splendid views along the cliff-top coastal walk.

In spring and summer this area is rich in nesting sea birds, including cormorant, shag, and kittiwake, and the moorland terrain of the cliff-top also attracts several interesting land birds and butterflies. In July and August there is a wonderful colour combination of purple heather and yellow gorse.

Walking up to Howth lighthouse, it is difficult to believe that Dublin is just a few miles away— until, that is, you see Dublin Bay spread out before you. On the beaches outside Howth (visible from the train) wading birds such as oystercatchers mingle with the human beachcombers.

There are a host of different sorts of tours by bus to various destinations (see page 126), details of which can be found at any of the Tourist Information Centres, Dublin Bus, or Busaras. Some destinations are even accessible by regular Dublin bus, though this may involve a walk at the end of the line.

Finally, this is the one time you may think it worthwhile to rent a car, in order to explore with some independence Dublin's wonderful and varied hinterland, which, among many splendid things, contains some of the finest houses and gardens you are ever likely to see.

Whatever you decide, here are some suggestions for excursions, all of which can be done in a day from the city. The list is not exhaustive, but it does include a wide variety of the main attractions you'll wish to see. (Detailed with each excursion are its location and, at the end of each entry, its opening hours, entrance fees, costs incurred, and access possibilities from Dublin.)

South of the City

County Wicklow, to the south of Dublin, rightly deserves the title of "Garden of Ireland." There you'll find some of the most spectacular scenery in the country, with rugged mountains, steep, wooded river valleys, and deep lakes. It also boasts some of the finest mansions and gardens of the old Ascendancy (see page 16), sandy beaches — **Sandymount Strand** is just a few minutes away from the Irish capital — and a host of charming villages.

James Joyce Museum
Sandycove, County Dublin.
This museum is possibly one of the most unusual small museums in and around Dublin, because it is housed in a Martello Tower. (A series of such towers, some 12 meters (40 feet) high and 2.5 meters (8 feet) thick, were constructed along the coast at the beginning of the 19th century to guard against invasion by Napoleon.)

The distinctive outline of Sandycove's Martello Tower, home to the James Joyce Museum.

Joyce actually lived in the tower very briefly, and it has the honour of being the location for the first chapter of *Ulysses*. Full of Joycean memorabilia (including his guitar and waist-coat), correspondence, and rare editions of books and manu-scripts, it is one of the main shrines for Joyce enthusiasts. Open April–October Monday–Saturday 10:00 A.M.–5:00 P.M., Sunday 2:00–6:00 P.M.; or by arrangement, tel. 872 2077; adult fee: IR£2.40, children IR£1.15; combined ticket for Dublin Writers Museum and Shaw Birthplace IR£6.30, children IR£2.30; DART and bus no. 8.

Avoca Handweavers
Avoca Village, County Wicklow (also at Kilmacanogue, Bray).
A company of handweavers has been working here at Avoca since at least 1723, and visitors are able to watch them as they produce their beautifully coloured knitwear. There's a good café in the small complex of traditional buildings, and a shop. Monday–Friday 9:30 A.M.–5:30 P.M., Saturday–Sunday 10:00 A.M.–6:00 P.M.; car or bus tour.

Avondale House
Rathdrum, County Wicklow.
Around 1.5 km (1 mile) south of the village of Rathdrum lies Avondale, lifelong home of the great 19th-century politician

and statesman Charles Stewart Parnell (of the two overcoats; see page 18). The delightful house dates from 1779 and was restored in 1991 (the centenary of Parnell's death), so that now much of it is a museum of its former owner's life and times. The spacious, airy, and friendly rooms are restored to the decor of around 1850 and there is much Irish Chippendale and Hepplewhite furniture. Parnell's three-windowed bedroom looks out to spectacular views.

The estate surrounding the house, rich in wildlife, encompasses more than 202 hectares (500 acres), through which flows the Avondale River. The estate is actually a training school for the Irish Forest and Wildlife Service, so visitors can enjoy riverside nature trails and the acres of trees and shrubs. The Parnell Kitchen in the basement of the house sells light snacks. Open daily 11:00 A.M.–5:15 P.M.; guided tour IR£2.50, family ticket IR£6 (2 adults and 4 children), concessions; car park IR£1; car or bus tour.

Glendalough

County Wicklow.

An easy drive north of Rathdrum, Glendalough is one of the sacred sites of Ireland. It is also the place chosen by St. Kevin for a monastery which, over the centuries, became a great centre of learning and spirituality, attracting pilgrims from all over Europe. Why Glendalough was chosen is perhaps quite simple to imagine, for it is one of the most beautiful landscapes one could hope to see, with its clear lakes and streams surrounded by steep wooded hills.

Despite several Viking raids, a great fire at the end of the 14th century, and long years of neglect, many of the original buildings are still visible, and in common with religious sites everywhere (and despite the crowds in high summer) are still capable of inducing awe and veneration.

The excellent visitor centre provides useful information

on all aspects of the site in a 15-minute audio-visual and an exhibition of the history, geology, and wildlife of the area. Adults IR£2, children IR£1.

The site of Glendalough itself encompasses a roofless cathedral, an 11th-century round tower more than 30 meters (100 feet) high and 15 meters (50 feet) around the base, and a 9th-century barrel-vaulted church known as St. Kevin's Kitchen, while scores of Celtic crosses add their own particular eeriness to the landscape. Glendalough is open all day throughout the year from 9:30 A.M.; guided tours on request; visitor centre adults IR£1.50, children IR£1, concessions; car or bus tour.

Glendalough is part of the **Wicklow Mountains National Park**, which includes some spectacular scenery and wildlife, and through which, naturally enough, the Wicklow Way long-distance footpath wends its peaceful course.

Glendalough's three nature trails take less than an hour's relaxed walking and are well worth the effort — and this just a few miles away from Dublin.

Mount Usher Gardens
Ashford, County Wicklow.

More greenery is at hand near Ashford and a little farther along the River Vartry. The spectacular Mount Usher Gardens were first established in 1868 by the Walpole family. The climate and soil are such that plants and trees that would not normally survive this far north are capable of flourishing, which explains the enormous variety of 4,000 to 5,000 plants, trees, and shrubs from all over the world.

The 8-hectare (20-acre) paradise attracts not just human visitors, but also a wide variety of birds and wildfowl. Open 17 March–November daily 10:30 A.M.–6:00 P.M.; get there by car or bus tour. There is a tearoom.

Powerscourt Estate

Enniskerry, County Wicklow.

This estate outside Enniskerry consists of 5,665 hectares (14,000 acres) hugging the River Dargle. The gardens (among the greatest in the world) take in a view of the Sugar Loaf Mountain as part of their design (the informal Japanese garden contrasts with the splendour of the main terraces). The enormous 18th-century house, probably the greatest in Ireland, was destroyed by fire in 1974. The newly renovated house will contain a restaurant and crafts shops.

The formal splendour of the grounds testify to an aristocratic desire to tame nature, but it is done with such confident arrogance and with such superlative results that one can only be thankful that the work was undertaken.

The broad, sweeping terraces of the gardens offer magnificent views; statuary rears up out of ornamental lakes; deer roam the parklands; and the Dargle obligingly throws itself over 122 meters (400 feet) of rock to form the highest waterfall in Ireland (4 km/2½ miles from the main estate). There is a café, shop, and garden centre, all only 18 km (12 miles) from Dublin.

Open March-October every day 9:30 A.M.–5:30 P.M.; November–March every day 10:30 A.M.–dusk. Admission: house and garden, adults IR£4.00, children IR£3.00; garden only, adults IR£3.00, children IR£2.00. Guided tours available.

Russborough House

Blessington, County Wicklow.

This magnificent Georgian-Palladian house, built in 1740-1750 and designed by Richard Castle, is one of the best houses you will see in Ireland. It is constructed on a monumental scale, with a 213 meter (700 foot) façade, Doric arcades, and wonderful ornamentation, all set against a terraced landscape.

The magnificent interiors feature superb plasterwork by the Francini brothers, identifiable, as elsewhere, by their trademark of the eagles' heads. Their Irish apprentices cut their teeth on the extraordinary plasterwork on the staircase, which boasts increasingly lavish swags of flowers gently held in the mouths of some very patient-looking dogs. The inlaid floors are particularly lovely, and there are extensive collections of furniture, silver, tapestries, and carpets.

To top it all, the house harbours the invaluable treasure of the Beit Collection of paintings (shared with the National Gallery), which includes works by masters such as Gainsborough, Goya, Guardi, Hals, Reynolds, Rubens, Ruysdael, Velasquez, and Vermeer, and a wonderful series of eight paintings by Murillo depicting the story of the prodigal son.

Outside, the grounds cover some 80 hectares (200 acres). The house is open daily June–August 10:30 A.M.–5:30 P.M.; on Sundays 10:30 A.M.–5:30 P.M. Easter–May and September–October; admission fee adults IR£3, children IR£1; concessions; car or bus tour.

WEST OF THE CITY

Castletown House
Celbridge, County Kildare.
When one William Conolly, Speaker of the House of Commons, set his heart on a palatial country home, he turned to Italian architect Alessandro Galilei, who began to design this Palladian masterpiece.

Work began in 1719, and the design was finished by Irishman Edward Lovett Pearce, after Galilei had returned to Italy. The result is one of the very finest and most distinctive houses in Ireland. The entrance hall is vast; the famous Long Gallery has Pompeian-fresco inspired designs and Venetian chandeliers; the great staircase is the work of Simon Vierpyl; and the fabulous plasterwork is by the Francinis. There is also a charming print room (all the rage at the time).

The peaceful Botanic Gardens delight the eye.

The building is equipped with furniture and paintings of the era and the grounds (now sadly encroached upon) are adorned by a 48 meter (140 foot) high obelisk covered in a surprising combination of pineapples and eagles (visible on the horizon from the Long Gallery). Open April–October Monday–Friday 10:00 A.M.–6:00 P.M., Saturday 11:00 A.M.–6:00 P.M., and Sunday 2:00–6:00 P.M.; November–March Sunday 2:00–6:00 P.M.; admission fee adults IR£2.50, children IR£1; car or bus 67/67A followed by a ½-mile walk.

Irish National Stud
Tully, County Kildare.

All Ireland loves a horse, and County Kildare can claim to be at the heart of Ireland's obsession. The Curragh and Punchestown racecourses are here, and the National Stud has produced some of the most successful horses in Ireland. Visitors can see horses being trained and exercised. There is also a museum illustrating the history of the horse in Ireland (including the skeleton of the legendary racehorse Arkle). Open all year Monday–Friday 10:00 A.M.–5:00 P.M., Saturday 10:00 A.M.–6:00 P.M., Sunday 2:00–6:00 P.M.; admission fee adults IR£4, children IR£2; combined ticket covers Irish Stud, Irish Horse Museum, and Japanese Gardens.

NORTH OF THE CITY

Of all the areas accessible from Dublin in a day, it is perhaps north of the city that the visitor can gain most insight into Ireland's long and troubled history. It is here that the River Boyne flows, a river that has played such an important part in the nation's psyche and has witnessed so much over thousands of years.

National Botanic Gardens
Dublin City.

Originally modelled on London's gardens at Kew, Ireland's premier horticultural attraction was established by the Royal Dublin Society in 1795. With over 20,000 species roaming in more than 20 hectares (50 acres) of grounds, there is plenty to see and enjoy. The most spectacular feature is arguably the series of enormous conservatories containing plants such as orchids, palms and cacti, and the Curvilinear Range, a magnificent curving glasshouse of cast iron.

There are all sorts of different gardens and landscapes to explore, including a riverside walk. This is an oasis of peace, with views of the mountains and city landmarks. Gardens open May-September Monday-Saturday 9:00 A.M.–6:00 P.M., Sunday from 11:00 A.M.–6:00 P.M.; October-April Monday-Saturday from 10:00 A.M.–4:30 P.M., Sunday 11:00 A.M.–4:30 P.M.; free; bus 13, 19, 34.

Casino at Marino
Dublin City.

Around 4.5 km (3 miles) north of Dublin on the Malahide road is Lord Charlemont's "marine villa," built in 1762-1777. Designed by Sir William Chambers (and generally regarded as his masterpiece), it is considered to be one of the finest buildings of the period in Europe, and certainly one of the most fascinating and intriguing, with all sorts of humorous touches and deceptions.

The Casino looks like a single-storey building from the outside but is in fact three stories high and contains 8 rooms. The floors and plasterwork are exquisite, but perhaps it is the external craftsmanship that makes the building so satisfying, with sculpture and stone carving perfectly modified to the harmonies of the design (the urns on the roof are disguised chimneys). Restored beginning in the mid-1970s after years of neglect and opened to the public in 1984, the Casino, though surrounded on all sides by ill-planned encroachments, still stands in perfect splendour on a gentle rise.

Down the road is "Spite Crescent" (look for it if you go past in the bus), built by an enemy of Lord Charlemont to spoil his view from the Casino. It was here that Bram Stoker later wrote *Dracula* (1897). Casino open daily from June–September 9:30 A.M.–6:30 P.M., Wednesday and Sunday October– May noon–4:00 P.M. (tel. 833 1618); admission fee adults IR£2, children IR£1, concessions; multilingual guidebooks available; bus 20A, 20B, 27, 27A, 27B, 32A, 42, or 42B.

Malahide Castle
Malahide, County Dublin.

Parts of this crenellated castle, which was the home of the Talbot family for 800 years, date back to the 12th century. Consequently, it has an atmosphere all of its own (augmented reputedly by two ghosts — one of them a medieval retainer — plus some oak panelling) and has the added benefit of part of the National Portrait Collection, donated by the National Gallery, as well as much interesting 18th-century furniture. The house is hugely enjoyable, with its rich orange interior walls, a Chinese carpet and views of the grounds and distant mountains, particularly from the airy turret rooms.

James Boswell, biographer of Samuel Johnson, was married to a Talbot, and many of his papers were discovered this century at the castle. As well as audiotape tours in several languages (activated by a button in each room), there is also a craft shop and an excellent restaurant and imaginative café on the ground floor.

The surrounding park includes the Talbot Botanic Gardens (May–September 2:00–5:00 P.M., guided tours on Wednesday) with thousands of plant species, and the Fry Model Railway Museum, Ireland's largest O-gauge model railway, which children adore.

Castle open all year Monday-Friday 10:00 A.M.–5:00 P.M.; Saturday and Sunday 2:00–5:00 P.M.; adults IR£2.95, children IR£1.60, family ticket IR£7.95, concessions; combined ticket for castle and model railway adults IR£4.70, children IR£2.35, family ticket IR£11.75, concessions; car or bus 42 (also stops at Marino Casino).

Newbridge House and Victorian Farm
Donabate, County Dublin.

Down the social scale a little from the mansions and palaces you may have seen already, Newbridge House and its estate of 142 hectares (350 acres) belonged to the Cobbe family from 1736. The beautifully restored house contains some interesting furniture and plasterwork, and there is also a museum of rural life incorporating artisans' cottages with period furniture and tools.

Open April to September Tuesday-Friday 10:00 A.M.–5:00 P.M., Saturday 11:00 A.M.–6:00 P.M., Sunday 2:00–6:00 P.M.; adults IR£2.75, children IR£1.50, family ticket IR£7.50 (family ticket for Newbridge, Malahide castle IR£11.75), concessions; car.

Newgrange
Slane, County Meath.

Roughly 3 km (2 miles) east of Slane, this is quite definitely the most spectacular of the prehistoric sites around Dublin and built on a massive scale in every sense: 500 years older than the Pyramids (3000 B.C.), this huge mound, (nearly 12 meters, some 40 feet high and almost 90 meters/300 feet wide) is constructed from 200,000 tons of stone, much of which was somehow or other hauled from the Wicklow Mountains and the Mountains of Mourne (the largest stones weigh around 10 tons).

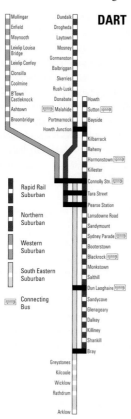

Used as a crematorium and tomb, it was richly decorated with abstract stone carving which can still be seen (a huge decorated stone guards the entrance). The most incredible feature of Newgrange, however, is that the whole edifice is aligned in such a way that during the winter solstice, light from the sun floods the inner chamber for approximately 17 minutes — the guide attempts to reproduce this effect by plunging the chamber in total darkness and slowly bringing up the lights.

The guided tour takes visitors into the heart of the barrow via an extremely narrow, low passage. Newgrange can get very crowded indeed and there can be long waits for the tour, so try to get there early or consider going out of season unless you are on a Bus Eireann bus tour which secures you privileged access. Admission fee adults IR£3, children IR£1.25, family ticket IR£7.50.

Nearby is Knowth (also a bus tour destination), an even larger complex which is still being excavated; until recently, visitors were not allowed inside. Open daily November–February 10:00 A.M.–4:30 P.M.; March and April 10:00 A.M.–5:00 P.M.; May 9:30 A.M.–6:00 P.M.; June–September 9:30 A.M.–7:00 P.M.; October 10:00 A.M.–5:00 P.M.; guided tours during opening times; adults IR£2, children 50p, family ticket IR£5, concessions; car or bus tour.

Tara

County Meath.

Tara is probably the most evocative name in Irish history. Not much remains now of the hill of kings and the capital of the ancient kingdoms of Ireland, but the magic of the place is if anything enhanced by the absence of tangible sights.

The audio-visual is shown in a 19th-century church with an Evie Hone stained-glass window depicting the coming of the Holy Spirit. Afterwards, the guided tour takes you to the hill itself, from where (it is claimed) you can see 12 counties. The lines of the earthworks are still visible, as is a burial chamber, and the chariot stone, an upright stone against which the chosen high king of Tara is said to have ridden his chariot wheels to hear the stone cry out its confirmation of his kingship. Open every day, mid-June to mid-September 9:30 A.M.–6:30 P.M.; May to mid-June and mid-September to October 9:30 A.M.–5:30 P.M.. Adults IR£1, children 40p, concessions; car or bus tour.

WHAT TO DO

Dublin bustles by day and comes alive at night, so there is plenty to enjoy when your sightseeing is done. With first-class shops and a profusion of booksellers, galleries, and antique dealers, you can browse or buy contentedly. If you're feeling active, there are excellent opportunities for sports, while Dublin's nightclubs will keep you busy till the early hours. What's more, the city's many pubs are the mainstay of social life, offering conversation and a quiet pint, food, music, and song. For at-a-glance information on the city's entertainment facilities, refer to the map on the cover of this guide.

SHOPPING

Opening hours (see page 121) vary considerably, with newsagents and sandwich bars open well before 9:00 A.M. and other stores just getting going by 9:30 or 9:45 A.M. Most are closed by 5:30 to 6:00 P.M., but on Thursday there is late-night shopping until 8:00 P.M. The majority of shops are closed all day Sunday.

If you buy anything to take home with you, you should be entitled to a refund of VAT (sales tax) within two months of the purchase, though EU nationals have to spend at least IR£41. This can be done by taking a validated store receipt either to the special Cashback desk or to the customs officials at your airport or ferry terminal of departure. Look for a special notice in the store window, or ask a sales assistant. Identification is required.

Stores and Shops

The main shopping areas and centres are in and around Grafton Street, St. Stephen's Green, Temple Bar, O'Connell Street and Henry Street. The department stores are in Grafton Street (**Brown Thomas**, excellent for Irish fashion design, has now relocated to the former Switzers building) and O'Connell Street (**Clerys**, for the more budget-conscious).

Shopping malls include the **St. Stephen's Green Shopping Centre**, the largest in the city, which is a bright and spacious shopping arena where you can buy just about anything and also have a meal (it can be very crowded, especially in summer). The **Powerscourt Townhouse** on Clarendon Street (follow the sign on Grafton Street) is on a smaller scale and specializes in wonderful restaurants, cafés, crafts, jewellery, and clothes stores. Also on Clarendon Street is the secretive **Westbury Mall**, which has cafés and gift shops.

On the other side of Grafton Street in Dawson Street is the **Royal Hibernian Way**, a small shopping mall with some very exclusive clothes shops. Finally, there is the **ILAC Centre**, which is second only to St. Stephen's Green. Here you'll find many clothes stores for all ages and a large branch of **Dunnes Stores**, an Irish clothes and food shop chain.

Branches of **Marks & Spencer** can be found in Grafton Street and Henry Street, where most of the larger chain-stores are represented, including the **Body Shop** for natural beauty products, **HMV** for music and concert tickets and **The Levi Store** for casual clothing.

Of course, Dublin wouldn't be Dublin without its markets, and one of the best is **Mother Redcap's** in Back Lane (opposite Christ Church Cathedral). This wonderful indoor market has stalls selling clothes and music, books and antiques, as well as excellent cheeses, pastries, and cakes (try **The Gallic Kitchen**, just inside the entrance). If you're looking for bargain secondhand clothes, try the **Iveagh Market**, next door to Mother Redcap's.

Good Buys

Antiques: Everywhere you go you will come across antiques shops and stalls, and one of the most famous "antiques highways" is Francis Street (Dublin 7). This has many fine art and antique stores, but you stand more chance of a bargain in Bachelors Walk and Ormond Quay on the Liffey.

Art: There are some excellent private art galleries in Dublin, many specializing in the work of contemporary Irish artists. The Oriel Gallery in Clare Street (next door to Greene & Co. bookshop) has many fine works, particularly from the early 20th century, while the Temple Bar Gallery in Temple Bar exhibits the work of up to 40 resident artists. The Solomon Gallery (Powerscourt Townhouse) displays the work of contemporary Irish artists.

Books: Dublin has many fine bookshops, of the general and specialist, new and secondhand types. Some of the best include Waterstone's and Hodges Figgis (of Ulysses fame), in Dawson Street, both of which have sections on Irish interests, and the Dublin Bookshop in Grafton Street. Fred Hanna's in Nassau Street sells new and secondhand books, posters and old postcards, and International Books in South Frederick Street specializes in languages. If you're interested in antiquarian books, go to Cathach Books in Duke Street. The Irish Film Centre in Eustace Street houses a bookshop devoted to all things cinematic and televisual, and in Temple Bar are George Webb's Bookshop (Crampton Quay) and Cathair Books (Essex Gate). Greene & Co. in Clare Street has new and secondhand books; Eason's on Lower O'Connell Street is a huge general bookshop with a large periodicals and international press section. The Winding Stair on Ormond Quay is a popular, labyrinthine secondhand bookshop with a café.

Golf is something of an obsession in Ireland, and visiting players are welcome.

Chocolates: Exquisite Belgian handmade chocolates are on sale at Leonidas in the Royal Hibernian Way and in Mary Street; their Irish equivalents are at Butler's Irish Chocolates in Grafton Street.

Crafts: The Irish Craft Council Gallery at the top of the Powerscourt Townhouse Centre is a wonderful introduction to contemporary Irish crafts. In Nassau Street the Kilkenny Shop (pottery) and Blarney Woollen Mills offer a vast range of Irish goods. The Tower Design Centre on Pearse Street, off Grand Canal Quay, has a range of crafts made and sold on the premises.

Crystal: Waterford, Cavan, Galway, Tipperary, and Tyrone Crystal is sold everywhere, and prices do not vary, so just choose your favourite design.

Food: Dunnes Stores (ILAC Centre) sell Irish smoked salmon (ask for the wild, not farmed, variety), and you might also try McConnell & Nelson in Royal Hibernian Way, who will send salmon overseas. Mother Redcap's Market has a treasure in The Gallic Kitchen, and the Bretzel Bakery (Lennox Street, Portobello) is a superb kosher bakery with delicious bagels.

Footwear: Try the Natural Shoe Store in Drury Street and Tutty's (Powerscourt Townhouse), who make exclusive tailor-made shoes. Grafton Street also has a good concentration of shoe shops.

Knitwear: Bargains are to be had here. Try Blarney Woollen Mills (Nassau Street), Dublin Woollen Mills (Lower Ormond Quay), and The Sweater Shop (Wicklow Street). Bright contemporary knitwear is sold in Tricot Marine in Grafton Street; Inisfree Handknits can be bought direct from the manufacturers at number 26 Merrion Square.

SPORTS

Jogging is quite usual in Dublin, particularly in the suburbs. The best place to go for true fellow solidarity is Phoenix Park, where you can relax and watch sports, especially on weekends.

There aren't very many **tennis** courts in Dublin, but if you want a game, the best place to try is Herbert Park in Ballsbridge, where you can either book or try to arrive before the early-evening rush.

Golf is extremely popular in Ireland and there are many superb courses in and around Dublin; these rarely require advance booking. Telephone the Golfing Union of Ireland at 269 4111 for information.

Fishing is also an Irish obsession. Sea angling is permitted all year round, but river fishing requires a licence (ask at any fishing shop). Tourist information supplies *The Anglers'' Guide to Dublin*.

Greyhound racing is on at Shelbourne Park, Ringsend, and at Harold's Cross Stadium; **horseracing** takes place at Leopardstown and The Curragh. **Rugby** and **soccer** are played at the Lansdowne Road venue in Ballsbridge, and traditional **hurling** at Croke Park.

There are opportunities for all sorts of **watersports** along Dublin's coastline, and there are fine beaches at Malahide, Dollymount, Portmarnock, and Donabate in the north, and Sandymount, Sandycove, Bray, and Killiney in the south. It is not advisable to swim within 8 km (5 miles) of the city centre because of pollution.

For all sports, Dublin Tourism can provide visitors with any necessary information.

ENTERTAINMENT
Music

The word *Seisiún* — meaning an impromptu evening of music and song, usually in a pub — has a particular resonance for the Irish, and there is plenty of opportunity in Dublin to enjoy traditional Irish sounds. A session starts when someone — usually the innocent-looking man sitting in the corner huddled over a pint of Guinness — produces a guitar as if from nowhere, and his neighbour responds by bringing out a well-concealed *bodhrán* (traditional Irish drum). Soon everyone is joining in.

Some pubs and hotels stage organized sessions, but the real fun is when the musicians are spurred on by the enthusiastic response of the audience. Local newspapers and listings magazines (see page 117) give details of other locations.

Symphonic and **chamber music** can be heard at the year-round programme of concerts at the National Concert Hall (NCH) in Earlsfort Terrace. Classical, chamber, and modern music can also often be heard in the beautiful surroundings of the Royal Hospital, Kilmainham, and in the homes and castles surrounding Dublin in the GPA "Music in Great Irish Houses" festival (in mid-June). Churches like St. Anne's Church (see page 29) often give lunchtime recitals and concerts, details of which can be found on noticeboards outside or in the vestibule. Look too for recitals and concerts at the Bank of Ireland Arts Centre in Foster Place.

Opera can really only be heard at the National Concert Hall and in the spring and winter seasons of the Dublin Grand Opera Society at the Gaiety Theatre in King Street. The NCH also holds evenings of **jazz** and Gilbert and Sullivan.

No visitor to Dublin should miss an evening of music and conversation at a traditional pub.

The Royal Dublin Society in Ballsbridge is the venue for huge open-air concerts, including **rock** of the calibre of U2 and traditional Irish music and jazz. The *Irish Times* carries a diary and advertisements for all such events, and you can

CALENDAR OF EVENTS

For the most up-to-date information consult Dublin Tourism and local listings (see page 117).

January — *International Rugby Championships*: Lansdowne Road and various other venues.

February/March — *Dublin Film Festival*: Films, seminars, and lectures at various cinema venues.

March — *St. Patrick's Day Parade*: Marching bands from all over the world and live music in a festive atmosphere.

March/April — *Dublin Feis Ceoil*: RDS, Ballsbridge, Dublin 4. Traditional music festival.

April/May — *Festival of Early Irish Music*: Venues throughout Dublin. Performances and workshops.

May — *Spring Show & Garden Festival*: RDS, Ballsbridge, Dublin 4.

June — *GPA Music in Great Irish Houses*: International music festival in the Dublin area's houses and castles.

Bloomsday: Dublin city centre. Celebration of Joyce and *Ulysses* in city streets and parks, and at the oyce Museum, Sandycove.

Irish Derby: The Curragh, Co. Kildare.

June-August — *Irish Studies Summer School*: Trinity College, Dublin 2, University College, Dublin, and St. Patrick's College, Maynooth. Residential courses for all interests and ages.

July — *Pipe Band Championships*: Various venues.

Dalkey Festival: Dalkey (served by DART).

Dun Laoghaire Festival: Dun Laoghaire. Parades, music, sports events (served by DART).

James Joyce Summer School: University College, Dublin 2. Joycean studies and celebration.

Blackrock Summer Festival: Blackrock (served by DART).

August — *Dublin Horse Show*: RDS, Ballsbridge, Dublin 4. International equestrian event.

September — *All-Ireland Hurling & All-Ireland Football Finals*: Croke Park, Dublin 3.

October — *Dublin Theatre Festival*: Dublin City.

consult local papers and listings magazines for up-to-the-minute information (see page 117).

During the summer months, the streets around Temple Bar and Grafton Street are replete with buskers of all sorts and degrees of talent, and there are often lunchtime performances in the shelter of the bandstand in St. Stephen's Green.

Film

There are popular cinemas all over Dublin showing the latest mainstream releases (see map), with O'Connell Street the main city-centre area.

Important cinemas for the less commercial art-house and limited circulation films from around the world include the Irish Film Centre in Eustace Street, the Lighthouse Cinema in Middle Abbey Street, and The Screen in Townsend Street. Outside the centre there are some newer multi-screen cinema complexes like the 12-screen cinema at The Square, Tallaght, and the 10-screen cinema centre at Coolock.

Theatre

Dublin has a proud and radical tradition in theatre which is still very much alive, so advance booking is advisable (apply to the theatre itself).

The **Abbey Theatre** in Lower Abbey Street is Ireland's national theatre. It contains two stages, with the intimate Peacock usually the more radical and experimental of the two — you'll find it in the basement. The **Gate Theatre** in Parnell Square has a similar tradition, with an emphasis on Irish and international theatre, as well as Shakespearian plays. The **Olympia** in Dame Street is the venue for all sorts of popular theatre and variety shows, and also doubles as a concert hall, while a similar mix of theatre, ballet, and revue is staged at the **Gaiety Theatre** in South King Street.

The **Project Arts Centre** in East Essex Street specializes in modern experimental work and doubles as a gallery during the day. The **City Arts Centre** in Moss Street is a lively venue for theatre and art exhibitions.

Both the **Andrews Lane Theatre** and the **Riverbank Theatre** (at Merchant's Quay) show international contemporary work. Look for special productions at the Bank of Ireland Arts Centre in Foster Place, Tivoli Theatre, Dublin Castle, and Trinity College.

Nightclubs

As in every other city, nightclubs come and go with bewildering speed, so it is essential to check local listing publications (see page 117). Virtually every type of music can be heard somewhere, any night of the week, so persevere.

Premises are often taken over for the same purpose and quite a few can be found in the Leeson Street area. Annabels is a trendy club and disco located beneath the Burlington Hotel in Leeson Street. Others to look for in Temple Bar are Club M in Anglesea Street, Rock Garden in Crown Alley, and Bad Bob's Backstage Bar in East Essex Street. Henry's, at the Henry Grattan lounge in Baggot Street, also happens to serve good food. Busloads of people flock to hear middle-of-the-road Irish cabaret at Jury's Hotel in Ballsbridge and Doyle's Irish Cabaret in the Burlington Hotel in Leeson Street.

CHILDREN'S DUBLIN

Children are well catered to in Dublin and many of the things that you want to do — trips out to the beach and jaunts into the mountains — will also appeal to young ones. Here, however, are a few more ideas for city-based activities:

Museums: Fry Model Railway Museum at Malahide Castle will delight aspiring engine drivers young and old, while the

National Wax Museum has a special "Children's World" tableau depicting well-known fairy-tale characters. Older siblings should enjoy the tour of Dublin Castle, especially the ancient Viking defences.

Parks and Zoos: Nature trails through Phoenix Park (see page 41) will keep all budding botanists happy, while Dublin Zoo, situated within the park, has a pet corner and zoo train especially designed for younger children.

Restaurants: Many restaurants and cafés positively welcome children, and some offer special children's menus at slightly lower prices. Among the best are Chompy's in the Powercourt Townhouse Centre, the Kilkenny Kitchen in Nassau Street (which provides high chairs), and The Bistro Pizza and Pasta restaurant in Castle Market, which provides pens and colouring books.

Fitzer's Café in the National Gallery also has high chairs. The Coffee Dock Grill in Jury's Hotel, Ballsbridge, provides special children's menus, as do some pub restaurants, such as O'Dwyer's in Lower Mount Street (see page 142).

Transport: Family tickets are available for rail and bus services and offer a substantial saving on regular fares. Children under 16 travel at half the adult fare on buses and less than half on the DART.

Tours: The self-guided Rock-'n' Stroll Trail around Dublin, which follows in the footsteps of Irish rock legends, will appeal to teenagers interested in the contemporary rock scene.

Come here often? An inhabitant of Dublin Zoo pauses obligingly for photographs.

DINING OUT

Anyone with the idea that Irish cuisine is a contradiction in terms will have their notions rudely shattered when they come to Dublin. The days of overcooked cabbage, mountains of potatoes, and calorie-laden puddings smothered with cream have been largely superseded by a new era of refinement, in which excellent basic ingredients are handled with greater delicacy and lightness of touch. Of course, traditional Irish dishes such as boxty and colcannon (see page 96–97) are still featured on many menus, but a new cuisine born out of exposure to higher European standards has led to the imaginative use of low-fat alternatives and healthier cooking methods.

Situated as it is on the broad sweep of Dublin Bay, with the waters of the Atlantic nearby, Dublin not suprisingly exploits its natural advantages, offering a tantalizing range of fresh fish and seafood dishes. You can choose anything from succulent langoustines to freshly caught lobster and crab, wild salmon, sole, and plaice. Even the most humble cod, coated in a rich batter and served with chips, can be one of the most sublime delights when eaten in the bracing breeze along Howth seafront.

From high-class French restaurants to cosy ethnic cafés, whatever your tastes, you're certain to find something to suit them in Dublin.

Meal Times

Most hotels and restaurants serve breakfast from 6:00 or 7:00 A.M. until about 10:00 A.M., while lunch is usually from about 12:30 P.M. until 2:00 or 3:00 P.M. Many pubs tend to get crowded with office-workers at lunchtime, so it's best to arrive early. Cafés serve snacks and light meals all day from 8:30 or 9:00 A.M. until 6:00 P.M., though many stay open until as late

Whether you plan to eat or simply drink and talk, it's wise to arrive early at the pub.

as 1:00 or 2:00 A.M. Some restaurants open for evening meals only, usually from about 6:00 P.M. until 11:30 P.M., although many Chinese and Indian establishments stay open until the early hours of the morning.

Most Dubliners prefer to dine after 8:00 or 8:30 P.M., so if you haven't booked your place at a restaurant in advance, you stand more chance of finding a table if you set out early. It's always wise to make a reservation, especially for the expensive restaurants, where they are usually *de rigueur*.

Breakfast is either the "continental" variety — fruit juice, rolls, coffee or tea — or traditional Irish, which generally means robust portions of fried egg, bacon, tomatoes and sausages, bread or toast, all washed down with gallons of strong tea.

Lunch can be as filling or as light as you like it, depending on where you choose to eat. Many of the more expensive restaurants offer set three- or four-course lunches, but you can also order simple salads, sandwiches, or a selection of hot or cold main meals at most pubs, cafés, or snack-bars. In the evening the *table d'hôte* menus provide the best value for money, offering set three- or four-course meals for a fixed price. If you prefer not to have an appetizer or dessert, you are better off selecting individual dishes from the *à la carte* menu. It's also worth remembering that value added tax on wine adds considerably to the final bill.

WHERE TO EAT

For a selection of some of the best eating establishments in Dublin, see our list of recommendations starting on page 137. The choice ranges from elegant restaurants where you can linger over a sumptuous five-course dinner to the humble chips shop offering crispy batter-coated portions of tasty fish and chips wrapped in newspaper to take away.

Cafés of all shapes and sizes abound in Dublin; dining out is one of the city's pleasures.

In between there's an infinite variety of ethnic restaurants, cafés, self-service snack-bars and pubs, each with their own distinctive ambience. Inevitably, standards of service can vary considerably from one place to the next, and while the majority of establishments are welcoming and friendly, there are some that are not.

If you want to dine inexpensively in historic splendour, Trinity College Dining Hall fits all your require-

ments. The beautiful oak-panelled refectory, damaged by fire in
1984 but since exquisitely restored, has long trestle tables over-
looked by sombre portraits of long-gone college luminaries —
a splendid setting for consuming traditional Irish fare. For a little over the price of a pint of stout, you can eat here to your
heart's content between noon and 2:00 P.M. any day of the week.

Cafés provide an excellent place to sit and watch the
world rush by. Most Dubliners head for that veritable Dublin
institution, Bewley's Oriental Café in Grafton Street. There's
a faded charm about the place, and the stained-glass windows produce a suitably reverential atmosphere inside.

However, many museums and other attractions have far
superior cafés with a superb selection of hot meals and
snacks, so bear this in mind when planning your day. One of
the most delightful cafés is to be found in the Irish Film Centre, located in the trendy Temple Bar district, which offers
imaginative dishes in a relaxing setting. Another excellent
café-restaurant is located at the Irish Museum of Modern
Art, in the soothing atmosphere of the basement, while the
National Gallery museum café (an outlet of Fitzer's) is open
until 8:00 P.M. on Thursdays.

A favourite Dublin tradition is high tea in one of the city's
grand hotels. To the background strains of soothing Irish harp
or piano music, a liveried waiter will bring you a pot of
freshly brewed tea and a silver tray laden with dainty sandwiches, sweet cakes, and pastries while you recline in the
comfortable surroundings of the Shelbourne or the Gresham.
For sheer decadence, there's nothing to beat it.

Starters and Main Course

It's no surprise that **fish** and **seafood** figure largely on Dublin
menus, and not least in the range of starters (appetizers).
Wild Irish salmon tops the list. It can be poached or steamed

and served simply with a wedge of lemon. Alternatively, it can be smoked over oak branches, thinly sliced, and finely dressed with capers.

Dublin Bay prawns are also very popular as a starter and are served hot with warm butter or cold with a light cocktail dressing. However you choose to eat them, they are always plump, juicy, and delicious. Other types of seafood regularly served in the city's restaurants include Galway Bay oysters, mussels from Wexford, Donegal crab, and Dingle Bay lobster.

For the main course try some Irish **beef**, which may be served in a variety of guises. As well as the traditional steak or roast, the prevailing culinary climate has produced such adventurous gourmet delicacies as beef stuffed with oysters, stir-fried beef with ginger, fillets of beef with cream cheese and mushrooms, and, as you might expect, beef cooked in Guinness or Irish whiskey.

Alternatively, you could try some home-produced **lamb**, transformed into dishes which have given Dublin's top chefs a world-class reputation: roast leg of lamb with black olives and garlic, stuffed filet of lamb with apple and mint sauce, rack of lamb *persillade* (with chopped parsley) with courgettes ... the list is endless.

Ham and **pork** also feature strongly on Irish menus, from tender Limerick ham to plump and tasty sausages which serve as an accompaniment to salty home-cured bacon on the Irish breakfast table. **Chicken** is invariably home-reared, usually free-range and full of flavour. It may be served roasted, wrapped with bacon or ham and stuffed with a savoury herb filling, or, more exotically, as chicken breast wrapped around a salmon or walnut mousse and served with potatoes.

Traditional **Irish dishes** have not escaped the effects of *nouvelle cuisine*. Many restaurants have given old dishes a new twist, adapting ingredients and cooking methods to the new, lighter approach. Some dishes to look for include colcannon (mashed potatoes with leeks and cabbage), crubeens (pigs" trotters), coddle (boiled bacon, sausages, onions, and potatoes), boxty (a tasty potato pancake filled with meat, vegetables, or fish) and, of course, Irish stew, made with lamb, potatoes and vegetables.

Vegetarians are particularly well catered to in Dublin, and will quickly find some favourite eating establishments. There are quite a few specialist and semi-specialist vegetarian places, and most restaurants and cafés include several vegetarian options on the menu, though some may need a little advance warning.

For vegetarian dishes, you can choose between the exotic — vegetable couscous, or parsnips stuffed with brazil nuts and vegetables in a red pepper sauce — to the unspectacular, though equally delicious, tagliatelle with mushrooms and tomatoes (there are lots of Italian restaurants, always good for vegetarian options).

Snacks

There are many fast-food establishments in Dublin, and undoubtedly one of the most popular is The Gallic Kitchen, situated in Mother Redcap's Market, opposite Christ Church Cathedral. Instead of the usual tasteless pizza and burger in a bun found in other fast-food outlets, you can regale your taste-buds with succulent home-cooked salmon wrapped in flaky pastry, delicious quiches and pies, and some mouthwatering, calorie-laden chocolate cheesecakes.

There are also plenty of delicatessens and sandwich bars that cater to the quick business lunch trade, and many of these are very good indeed.

Most important for the visitor, perhaps, are the many excellent cafés and restaurants situated within museums and galleries, large country houses, and other similar attractions.

These can be invaluable, offering everything from pastries and snacks to quick lunches with wine. Pubs, too, often serve good food (see below), and all the usual fast-food outlets can be found in the centre of the city.

Desserts

Whatever your choice of dessert, you will always be asked if you want cream with it. Dubliners do like their cream, particularly when served with a big slab of apple pie, carrot cake, cheesecake, or one of the many delicious combinations of ice cream desserts. In fact, puddings in Ireland

---

Dublin Pubs

A visit to Dublin would be incomplete without getting to know some of its pubs, and whether it's drink, food, conversation, atmosphere, or music you're after, you're bound to find something to your liking. (The Shopping and Entertainment map on the cover of this guide pinpoints the establishments listed below.)

O'DWYER'S (Lower Mount Street) offers convivial conversation and good food, while MOTHER REDCAP'S TAVERN (Back Lane) is famed for music and storytelling. KITTY O'SHEA'S (Upper Grand Canal Street) is a glass-boothed memorial to Kitty and Parnell and serves excellent food; RYAN'S PUB (Parkgate Street) is all conversation and Victorian mahogany and brass. THE LONG HALL (South Great George's Street) is a Victorian time machine with (reputedly) the city's longest bar counter, while the BRAZEN HEAD (Lower Bridge Street) has music most evenings and a great atmosphere all the time (and it serves lunch).

DAVY BYRNES (Duke Street) was immortalized by being featured in *Ulysses*. BARRY FITZGERALDS (Marlborough Street) offers traditional Irish music, as does SLATTERY'S in Capel Street on Sunday afternoons. The OLIVER ST. JOHN GOGARTY (Fleet Street) offers good food and music. Find your favourite, and have fun in the process!

---

tend to be on the rich side, so be prepared for a major test of dietary resolve.

Drinks

Dublin would not be Dublin without the world famous stout, **Guinness**, which is available everywhere. It really does taste better in Dublin than anywhere else (a little smoother and less bitter), so do try it. Even in pubs it is usually brought to the customer a while after it

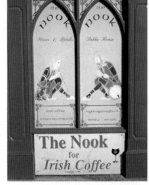

This cheerful taditional pub sign beckons you to eat, drink, and be merry.

has been ordered, because the pouring and settling process takes a little time, but it is well worth the wait. Other well-known Irish stouts like **Murphy's** are also available, and wherever you come from, you'll see plenty of beers you will recognize.

Spirits are available in profusion, and there is a great array of distinctive Irish **whiskeys** to choose from, some of the names of which you will see etched in the glass of pub windows. Generally it's cheaper to drink in pubs rather than hotel bars, and certainly more entertaining. Prices outside the city are also usually lower than in the city centre.

Wine is readily available, even in cheaper restaurants and cafés, with a particularly fine selection from the New World, such as Australian Chardonnays and Cabernet Sauvignons. Light Italian reds also feature prominently on the wine list. It is cheaper to order a half-liter or liter carafe of the house wine with your meal, but there are usually reasonable bottles at around IR£8-11.

INDEX

Where there is more than one set of references, the one in **bold** refers to the main entry, the one in *italic* to a photograph.

HANDY TRAVEL TIPS

An A–Z Summary of Practical Information

The telephone dialling code for the Dublin area from outside the city is 01; the code for Ireland is 353. All prices given in this book are in Irish pounds (IR£) and **not** UK Sterling.

A

ACCOMMODATION (See also YOUTH HOSTELS on page 128, and the selection of RECOMMENDED HOTELS starting on page 130)

Hotel accommodation in Ireland is classified by star ratings from one to five stars, and is registered and regularly inspected by the Irish Tourist Board (*Bord Fáilte*). The Tourist Board also publishes a list of approved hotel and guest house accommodation throughout Dublin, obtainable either through your local tourist information office (for addresses and phone numbers, see TOURIST INFORMATION OFFICES on page 123) or by contacting the **Irish Hotels Federation**, 13 Northbrook Road, Dublin 6, Ireland; tel. 497 6459, fax 497 4613.

All tourist information offices operate an accommodation reservation service, for which a small charge is made. It is always advisable to book accommodation in advance, especially if you plan to visit in the peak months of July and August.

Hotels generally offer a full range of services, including restaurants, licensed bars, currency exchange offices, gift shops, and lounges, while **guest houses** provide more limited facilities, but are of excellent value. Be aware that room prices quoted normally include government tax (VAT) of 12.5% but do not include service charges, which will add an extra 10-15% to your bill. Breakfast is often extra.

Details about **self-catering accommodation** in Dublin and the surrounding area can be obtained either from the Irish Tourist Board (which produces a complete illustrated guide) or from:

Irish Cottage Holiday Homes, 4 Whitefriars, Aungier Street, Dublin 4; tel. 475 7017, fax 478 5318.

Trident Holiday Homes, Unit 2, Sandymount Village Centre, Sandymount, Dublin 4; tel. 668 3534, fax 660 6465.

Dublin

Dublin also offers a variety of **college** and **university accommodation** when classes are not being held. Rooms and apartments at bargain rates are available for short stays on **Trinity College** campus between June and September. For further information, contact the Accommodation Office, Trinity College, Dublin 2; tel. 702 1023, fax 671 1267. **University College Dublin** provides a similar service. For further information, contact UCD Village, Belfield, Dublin 4; tel. 269 7696, fax 269 7704. Details of student accommodation can be obtained from the **Irish Student Travel Service**, 19 Aston Quay, Dublin 2; tel. 679 8833.

Holiday Hostels provides simple accommodation in dormitory-style rooms or shared bedrooms for visitors on a tight budget and are open all year round. For details of Holiday Hostels in Dublin, contact the Irish Tourist Board. Three places you can contact direct are:

Avalon House, 55 Aungier Street, Dublin 2; tel. 475 0001, fax 475 0303.

Kinlay House, 2-12 Lord Edward Street, Dublin 2; tel. 679 6644, fax 679 7437.

Marlborough Hostel, 81-82 Marlborough Street, Dublin 1; tel. 874 7629/874 7812, fax 874 5172.

AIRPORT

Dublin International Airport is a moderately sized modern complex offering a range of facilities, including a duty-free shopping centre, tourist information office, bank, bureau de change, post office, and branches of the major car rental firms.

The airport lies about 11 km (7 miles) north of the city centre and is well served by taxis and public transport (for fare information, see MONEY MATTERS on page 118) .

Dublin Bus operates a regular shuttle service between the airport (outside the main arrivals hall), the central bus station (Busaras), and major hotels in the city. Buses (41, 41A, 41B, 41C) leave every twenty minutes from early morning until midnight. Dublin Bus also provides daily bus transfers between the city centre, including Heuston railway station and Busarus, the provincial bus station, and Dublin airport.

Taxis line up outside the arrivals terminal.

B

BICYCLE RENTAL (See also PLANNING YOUR BUDGET on page 119)
What better way to explore Dublin's suburbs and the surrounding
countryside than by renting a bike? If you're flying to Dublin, you
can arrange to have your bicycle delivered to the airport.

Both identification and a minimum deposit of IR£40-50 are usually required when renting a bicycle. Contact Dublin Tourist Information or the Irish Tourist Board (see page 123) for further information
and a list of suggested sightseeing tours.

RailBike national bicycle rental is based on the rail network and allows you to collect and return bikes at any railway station. Rental
charges are about the same wherever you go, and there are several bicycle rental outlets throughout the city. Contact *RailBike*, 5 Leeson
Park, Dublin 6; tel. 497 1911, fax 497 0756, or look in the Golden
Pages of the telephone directory under "Bicycle Hire". Otherwise try:
McDonalds Cycles, 38 Wexford Street; tel. 475 2586.
Rent a Bike, 58 Lower Gardiner Street, Dublin 1;
tel. 872 5399.

C

CAR RENTAL (See also DRIVING on page 111 and PLANNING
YOUR BUDGET on page 119)
You can arrange to rent a car immediately upon arrival at Dublin
airport, or have one waiting for you if you book a fly-drive or rail-
sail-drive inclusive package. Alternatively, you can refer to the Gold-
en Pages of the telephone directory for addresses of leading firms.

To rent a car you'll need a valid driving licence held for at least
two years without endorsement. The minimum age varies from company to company and should be confirmed in advance. A deposit is
normally charged at the time of booking. Rental rates include third-
party fire and theft, but unless additional insurance is taken out in the
form of a collision damage waiver (CDW), in the event of an accident the renter is responsible for the first IR£900-1,350 of damage.

Dublin

CLIMATE

Dublin's climate is temperate, and contrary to popular belief, rain is not a permanent backdrop. The city experiences no violent extremes of temperature, thanks to the warming waters of the Gulf Stream, which influence much of the country. Of course, the weather is unpredictable, and you will certainly encounter rain or mist at whatever time of year you visit, so be prepared. Less rain falls on Dublin than on any other part of the country, however, and snow is uncommon in winter. The warmest months are July and August.

Average temperatures												
	J	F	M	A	M	J	J	A	S	O	N	D
°C	7	8	11	13	16	18	20	21	17	14	11	8
°F	45	46	52	55	61	64	68	70	63	57	52	46

Clothing. Dubliners are fashion-conscious people, and a certain standard of attire is expected in the exclusive hotels and restaurants. For everyday wear, be sure to pack clothing appropriate to the season: a heavy coat and sturdy shoes or boots in winter; lightweight garments, fold-up raincoat, and jacket in summer; and umbrella and sweater at all times. Evening temperatures on the sunniest summer days can be quite cool, and in spring there is often a chilling wind which takes the edge off the day's mild warmth.

Although the city is by no means prudish in its attitudes, it is advisable to observe an appropriate standard of dress when sightseeing in churches.

COMMUNICATIONS (See also TIME DIFFERENCES on page 122)

Post Offices. Mail boxes are painted green and have the word "post" in yellow on the top. Dublin's General Post Office is located at O'-Connell Street, Dublin 1; tel. 872 8888; it handles mail, public telex, telegrams, fax, and telephone services. If you don't know where you'll be staying in Dublin before you leave, you can arrange to have mail directed to you here, c/o Poste Restante. All poste restante mail will be held for two weeks, and the service is free for a maximum of three months. Take your passport or some other form of identification with a photograph when you go to collect your mail.

There is a post office at Dublin Airport. Postal charges to Britain and other EU member states are the same as internal rates. Many post offices exchange foreign currency and travellers cheques.

Telephones and Fax. The Irish telephone system (*Telecom Eireann*) has undergone extensive modernization, and both national and international communications are much improved. All areas of Ireland can be called without the operator and direct-dial international calls can be made from all hotels and most guest houses or from any public phone. Direct-dial calls from a pay phone are cheaper after 6pm Monday-Friday and on weekends. International calls are prefixed by the number 00, followed by the relevant country code. Bear in mind that any calls made from a hotel will have a hefty surcharge imposed.

The use of telephone cards is widespread in Dublin; you can buy them in units of 10, 20, 50, or 100 from post offices, newsstands or shops displaying a phone-card notice.

To call **directory inquiries**, dial 1190. Note that this service isn't free, but you are entitled to make up to three inquiries per call. The code for the **international operator** from a public phone is 114.

To send a telegram or fax, go to any post office or *Telecom Eireann* office. Faxes can be sent from public "copy centres." Alternatively, most hotels and many guest houses will have telex, fax, and photocopying facilities, which guests can use for a small charge.

Note. All of Dublin's telephone numbers have recently been changed from 6 digits to 7 digits. They are listed in the current Dublin area 01 telephone directory (found in main post offices and hotels). Assistance with new telephone numbers is available: dial freephone 1800 330 330 for help or information.

Dublin

COMPLAINTS

If something goes wrong that you cannot take care of yourself, report the matter to the Dublin Tourist Office (see page 124). In hotels and restaurants, discuss any problems with the proprietor or manager. A conciliatory tone and a quiet word can go a long way towards resolving problems.

CRIME (See also EMERGENCIES on page 113)

Compared to most urban centres, Dublin's crime rate is moderate, but it is, unfortunately, on the increase. Take sensible measures, such as leaving your valuables in the hotel safe. Be wary of pickpockets in crowded places, keep your wallet in an inside pocket, and don't leave objects unattended or open to view in a parked car. If you are robbed, report the incident to the hotel receptionist and the nearest police station. The police will provide you with a certificate to present to your insurance company, or to your consulate if your passport has been stolen. Be especially wary in the areas around St. Patrick's and Christ Church Cathedrals, and Summerhill.

Make photocopies of important documents such as passport, plane tickets, and so on, and keep them separately — they may facilitate replacements in case you lose your papers. Tourist information and some attractions provide a leaflet produced by *Gardai* (see POLICE on page 121): *A Short Guide to Tourist Security* (multilingual).

CUSTOMS and ENTRY FORMALITIES

For a stay of up to three months, a valid passport is sufficient for citizens of Australia, Canada, New Zealand, South Africa, and the USA. Passports are not required by British citizens born in the UK travelling from Britain.

As Ireland is part of the European Union (EU), free exchange of non-duty-free goods for personal use is permitted between Ireland and the UK. However, duty-free items are still subject to restrictions: check before you go.

For residents of non-EU countries, restrictions when returning home are as follows: **Australia**: 250 cigarettes **or** 250 g tobacco **or**

100 cigars; 1 l spirits **and** 1.5 litres wine; **Canada**: 200 cigarettes **and** 50 cigars **and** 400 g tobacco; 1.1 l spirits **or** wine **or** 8.5 l beer; **New Zealand**: 200 cigarettes **or** 50 cigars **or** 250 g tobacco; 4.5l wine **or** beer **and** 1.1 l spirits; **South Africa**: 400 cigarettes **and** 50 cigars **and** 250 g tobacco; 2l wine **and** 1 l spirits; **USA**: 200 cigarettes **and** 100 cigars **or** 2 kg tobacco, 1 l wine **or** spirits.

DISABLED TRAVELLERS

Efforts have been made to improve the city's accessibility to disabled travellers, and a number of hotels and guest houses have adapted their facilities to cater to visitors with special needs. However, many historic buildings and museums do not provide wheelchair ramps, and as in many other cities, there is still much to be done.

The National Rehabilitation Board, 25 Clyde Road, Dublin 4, tel. 668 4181, publishes an accommodation guide and fact sheets which indicate where wheelchair access and other facilities are available. Both are free and can be obtained from the Irish Tourist Board.

Disabled drivers resident in Britain can obtain special discounts on their vehicles on certain ferry crossings to Ireland. For details, contact the **Disabled Drivers' Association**, Brunswick Street, Dublin 7; tel. 872 1671. Leaflets are also available from all tourist information offices.

DRIVING

To enter Ireland with your own vehicle, you will need:

- a national driving licence (or an international driving permit for those coming from the USA, Australia, and South Africa)
- car registration papers
- a national identity sticker for your car
- a red warning triangle in case of breakdown
- insurance certificate valid for the Republic of Ireland

Insurance. You are advised to inform your insurance company of your travel plans, particularly if you want full comprehensive coverage. Note that your vehicle may not be driven by an Irish resident during your stay, with the exception of a garage mechanic with your written permission.

Driving conditions. Rush-hour traffic jams and limited parking space make driving in central Dublin an unpleasant experience. During the morning and evening rush hours, bottlenecks form rapidly, especially on the city's many bridges, but outside these times traffic is generally fluid. If you must drive in the city centre, try and plan your journey between 10am and 4pm to avoid the worst congestion.

Traffic in Dublin follows the same basic rules that apply in Britain. Drive on the left, pass on the right. Road signs are mostly bilingual. While Ireland is gradually converting to metric, you'll see both black-and-white signposts in miles and newer green ones in kilometers (Dublin's are almost entirely the latter). Seat belts in both the front and, where fitted, the back, must be worn, and children under 12 must travel in the rear. Ireland has very strict rules about drinking and driving; simply, do not do both.

Parking. Free parking on Dublin's streets during normal working hours is an impossibility. Expect to be towed away or heavily fined for parking illegally. Metered parking (for up to 2 hours) is quite limited, but you can often find a space. Your safest bet is to park in one of the multi-storey car parks, which are pin-pointed on the street map in *Tourism News*, issued free by Dublin Tourism and available at most hotels.

Speed limits. The speed limit is 90 k/h (55 mph) on all open roads and 112k/h (70 mph) on motorways. In town it is restricted to 50 k/h (30 mph). Cars towing trailers may not exceed 80 k/h (50 mph).

Breakdowns. If your car is rented, call the number given in the hire documents. If you are a member of an AIT driving club or the AA, call the Automobile Association of Ireland: *Irish AA Breakdown Service*: tel.1800-667 788.

Fuel and oil. There are filling stations everywhere, and many of them are self-service. A number are open 24 hours. Petrol (gasoline) is sold by the liter and comes in four grades: premium, super unleaded, diesel and unleaded. Unleaded petrol is widely available and is cheaper per liter than premium leaded.

Fluid measures

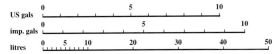

Distance

E

ELECTRIC CURRENT

Ireland's standard electrical supply is 220 volts 50 cycles AC. Plugs are 3-pin flat or 2-pin round. If you need a travel adaptor, bring one with you.

EMBASSIES and CONSULATES

Get in touch with the consulate of your home country if something disastrous happens — for example, if you lose your passport, get into trouble with the authorities or the police, or have an accident. The Consul can issue emergency passports, give advice on obtaining money from home, and provide a list of lawyers and doctors. It's best to phone in advance to check opening hours.

Australia:	Fitzwilton House, Wilton Terrace, Dublin 2; tel. 676 1517
Canada:	65 St. Stephen's Green, Dublin 2; tel. 478 1988
UK:	29 Merrion Road, Dublin 4; tel. 205 3700
USA:	42 Elgin Road, Dublin 4; tel. 668 8777

EMERGENCIES

(See also MEDICAL CARE on page 118 and POLICE on page 121)

In the event of an emergency, dial **999** for Police, Ambulance, Fire, and Coastguard. The call is free from all pay and card phones.

 G

GAY and LESBIAN TRAVELLERS
Gay Switchboard Dublin, Counselling Information, Old Doctors' Residence, Richmond Hospital, Dublin 7; tel. 872 1055.
Lesbian Line, 32 Upper Fitzwilliam Street, Dublin 2; tel. 661 3777.

GUIDES and TOURS
(See also PLANNING YOUR BUDGET on page 119)

By bus. City sightseeing tours by bus provide an excellent introduction to Dublin and the surrounding area, and there are a vast number to choose from:

Dublin Bus, 59 Upper O'Connell Street, Dublin 1; tel. 873 4222, the city's transport company, operates several guided tours. The *City Tour* takes in the principal sights including Trinity College, St. Patrick's and Christ Church Cathedrals, and Phoenix Park, and lasts approximately 2¼ hours. The tour is by open-top bus (the top deck is covered over in bad weather) and is also available in the evening during the summer. The *Heritage Tour* is more flexible, allowing you to explore the city's historic buildings and museums along the route. You purchase an all-day ticket and get on and off the bus as you please at any one of the 10 designated stops along the route. Daily excursions by double-decker bus along the north coast as far as Malahide and south coast as far as Delgany are available between May and September. *Irish Evening* trips offer a night of traditional music, song, and dance at the Irish Culture and Music Centre (*Cultúrlann na hÉireann*) in Monkstown. All bus tours depart from the Dublin Bus office, but free pick-up for morning tours are also available from many Dublin hotels.

Bus Éireann, Travel Centre, Busaras, Store Street, Dublin 1; tel. 836 6111, Ireland's national bus company, runs a city sightseeing tour as well as a number of other tours to the outlying attractions, including the Boyne Valley, Glendalough and Wicklow, and Powerscourt Gardens. All tours depart from the Travel Centre at Busaras.

Gray Line Tours, 3 Clanwilliam Terrace, Grand Canal Quay, Dublin 2; tel. 661 9666 offer, a range of excursions around Dublin and surrounding areas and a Night-Life tour including cabaret, and dinner and/or drinks at Jury's Irish Cabaret at Jury's Hotel or Doyle's Irish Cabaret at the Burlington Hotel. Tours depart from the Gray Line desk at the Dublin Tourism office and from a number of hotels.

By rail. Guided tours by rail along the length of the DART rail network (see page 124) from Bray to Howth are offered by **DART Tours**, 39 Shrewsbury Lawn, Dublin 4; tel. 2862861, and commentary is provided on points of historical or scenic interest on the way.

By foot. If you prefer to explore the city on foot, Dublin Tourism (see page 124) has signposted three self-guided **walking tours**, which you can enjoy at your own speed. The *Cultural Heritage Trail* covers Dublin north of the Liffey, while the *Old City Heritage Trail* heads east from Trinity College through Temple Bar to Dublin Castle. The *Georgian Heritage Trail* focuses on the city south of the river around St. Stephen's Green, Fitzwilliam and Merrion Squares, and includes the National Gallery, Museum, and Library. All three routes are best followed in conjunction with the detailed Heritage Trail booklets available from tourist information offices.

Rock'n'Stroll Trail, for **music** fans, points out places associated with such artists as Bob Geldof, U2, Sinead O'Connor, and the Chieftains, among others. Several themed walking tours are also arranged by various groups during the summer months, including the highly enjoyable *Dublin Literary Pub Crawl*, which comprises an evening of readings, song, and performance following in the footsteps of James Joyce, Samuel Beckett, Brendan Behan, *et al.* Contact Dublin Tourism (see p.age TK) for details.

Dublin Footsteps runs four 2-hour tours: a medieval walk, a literary walk, 18th-century Dublin, and a city centre walk. No booking is required and tours begin from Bewley's in Grafton Street or Mary Street. Telephone 496 0641/845 0772 or *Bord Fàilte* (see page 123). Historical walking tours of about two hours also begin from the front gate of Trinity College: for further information, phone 845 0241/453 5730.

Discover Dublin musical pub crawls start from Oliver St. John Gogarty pub in Temple Bar at 7:30pm every day (except Friday) from May to October. Literary Performance Tours take in Abbey Theatre, Trinity College, Dublin Castle, and medieval Dublin (tel. 478 0191). The Bank of Ireland at College Green produces a Sixty Golden Moments booklet, a self-guided historical walking tour.

By carriage. Get in touch with Dublin Horse-drawn Carriage Tours, St. Stephen's Green, Dublin 2; tel. 872 6968, whose tours come with commentary supplied by the driver. Carriages are lined up at the Grafton Street side of St. Stephen's Green, and itineraries and tour durations vary according to your preferences.

The standard of **guided tours** offered at most of Dublin's city and outlying attractions is extremely high. Many places precede tours with a short and informative audio-visual presentation, and in many attractions (such as Newman House, Dublin Castle, Russborough House) there is no other way of viewing interiors. The Irish Tourist Board can supply you with details of recommended agencies.

LANGUAGE

Ireland is officially bilingual and everyone speaks English. Signs are written both in English and Irish and are usually self-explanatory. On buses, *An Lar* means "City Centre."

LAUNDRY and DRY CLEANING

Having your laundry washed or cleaned by the hotel is the quickest and most convenient method, but prices are correspondingly high. If price is a consideration, it is worth seeking out a launderette or dry-cleaning establishment. Some cleaners offer a quick service, which takes a minimum of two hours and is slightly more expensive.

LOST PROPERTY

For property lost in public places, contact the police (*Gardai*) headquarters, Harcourt Square, Dublin 2; tel. 873 2222. If the item was lost on public transport or in a taxi, contact the relevant transport office or taxi company. If you lose your passport, notify the police and your consulate (see EMBASSIES AND CONSULATES on page 113) for emergency travel documents. For lost traveller's cheques, inform the police and the issuing company.

M

MEDIA

Radio and TV. The national broadcasting authority is RTE (*Radio Telefis Eireann*) which runs two TV channels, RTE1 and Network 2, and three radio stations, RTE1, 2FM, and *Radio na Gaeltachta* (in Irish). There are also smaller local stations. Television programmes from Britain via BBC and ITV (independent television) stations can be received in the Dublin area, as well as BBC Radio's stations 1, 2, 3, 4, and 5. Many hotels and some guest houses are equipped to receive satellite television programmes via CNN, Sky News, and other operators.

Newspapers and Magazines. Most newsagents stock the main UK national dailies and many sell American and European newspapers. Foreign newspapers and periodicals can be purchased at Easons, 40-42 Lower O'Connell Street, or at Bus Stop, 52 Grafton Street. For an authentic Irish experience, however, you should read the *Irish Times*, an excellent national daily with interesting articles and a useful *Notices* section. The *Irish Independent* has more Ireland-focused coverage and publishes a special Sunday edition.

A broad range of listings magazines gives an overview of events in Dublin. Publications such as *What's On in Dublin*, *Tourism News,* and *Tourism Dublin*, produced by the Irish Tourist Board, are comprehensive in their coverage and give useful restaurant reviews and up-to-date information on tourist attractions. *In Dublin* lists forthcoming festivals and events, while *Dublin Event Guide* is a free biweekly listings newspaper giving detailed coverage of what's on where.

MEDICAL CARE

Ask your insurance company if you are covered for medical treatment in Ireland. Visitors who are not reimbursed for medical bills abroad should take out a short-term holiday policy before setting out. Citizens of EU countries are covered by a reciprocal agreement and may use the Irish Health Services for medical and hospital treatment. Ask for the requisite forms at your local Social Security Office and, if you do need treatment when in Ireland, make it clear that you wish to be treated under the EU's social security regulations.

In the event of accident, dial **999** for an ambulance. Your hotel or guest house proprietor should be able to contact a doctor in an emergency. You can also contact the **Irish Medical Organisation** for a recommendation. Their address is 10 Fitzwilliam Place, Dublin 2; tel. 676 7273.

If you need emergency dental treatment, you should approach the **Irish Dental Association**, 10 Richview Office Park, Clonskeagh Road, Dublin 14; tel. 283 0499, which will be able to recommend a dentist.

Chemists (drugstores) are generally open during normal shopping hours. You can find the address of the nearest late-night **pharmacy** in the local press and under "Chemists — Pharmaceutical" in the phone directory. *O'Connell Pharmacy* at 55 Lower O'Connell Street is open Monday–Saturday 8:30am-10pm, and at 6 Henry Street, Dublin 1 until 8:30pm Thursday.

MONEY MATTERS

Currency. Ireland's monetary unit is the Irish pound (IR£), also known as the punt, and is divided into 100 pence (p). British and Irish money are not interchangeable. All prices given in this book are in Irish pounds.

Coins: 1p, 2p, 5p, 10p, 20p, 50p, and IR£1.

Notes: IR£5, IR£10, IR£20, IR£50, and IR£100.

Changing money. For the best exchange rate, visitors should change banknotes at banks and bureaux de change. The foreign exchange counter at Dublin International Airport is open daily 6:45am-10pm (9pm in winter).

Credit cards, traveller's cheques, Eurocheques. Credit cards are accepted in most hotels, restaurants, petrol stations, and large shops. Some guest houses may not accept credit cards, so be sure to ask before booking. Eurocheques are accepted provided they are supported by a valid Eurocheque card. Traveller's cheques supported by identification can be exchanged at most banks or main travel service offices.

Note. Personal cheques from a British bank account are not accepted anywhere.

PLANNING YOUR BUDGET

The following list will give you some idea of what prices to expect in Dublin. Due to inflation, however, they should only be considered as approximate. All prices given here and throughout the book are in Irish pounds and not UK sterling.

Airport transfer. Dublin Bus to Busaras (Central Bus Station) IR£2.50, taxi IR£12.

Bicycle rental. IR£7 per day, IR£30 per week (plus IR£40-50 refundable deposit).

Car rental. *Fiesta* or equivalent IR£30-35 per day, IR£125-250 per week. Rental rate includes third-party insurance, unlimited mileage, VAT, and passenger indemnity insurance, but excludes collision damage waiver (CDW).

Entertainment. Cinema IR£3-4, theatre IR£4-16, concert IR£10-30, nightclub IR£3-8 entrance.

Hotels (double room per night). Luxury class IR£155 upwards, first class IR£115-155, medium IR£65-115, budget class IR£65 or less.

Dublin

Meals and drinks. Breakfast IR£3-4, pub lunch IR£4.50, lunch or dinner for two in fairly good establishment IR£35, bottle of wine from IR£7, pint of beer IR£2, glass of Irish whiskey (40ml) IR£1.50, soft drink IR£1, coffee IR£1.

Museums. Admission is free for many museums and historic buildings, otherwise IR£1.50-2 adults, 60p-IR£1 children.

Petrol. 60p/litre; IR£2.65/gallon unleaded; IR£2.70/gallon leaded.

Public transport. One-day bus/rail ticket IR£4.50, one-day family bus/rail ticket IR£6, four-day Explorer ticket IR£10, weekly bus/rail ticket IR£14.50. Children under 16 pay half-price on the bus.

Shopping bag. Bread (800g) 65p, butter (454g) IR£1.50, margarine (454g) IR£1, Irish cheese (1kg) IR£5, potatoes (5kg) IR£4, salmon (per 454g) IR£5, tea (250g) IR£1.30, instant coffee (200g jar) IR£3.50, milk (1 litre) 60p.

Sightseeing. City Tour (2¼ hours) IR£8, Heritage Tour (all-day ticket) IR£5, North Coast Tour (2¾ hours) IR£8, South Coast Tour (3¾ hours) IR£9, Irish Evening tour (3½ hours) IR£10, Grand Tour of Dublin (full day) IR£16, evening tour IR£8. Reductions are available for children under 16.

Taxis. Initial charge IR£1.05 plus IR£1 per mile, minimum fare IR£3. A pick-up charge of IR£1.20 may be added if taxis are ordered. Negotiate fares for longer distance trips in advance.

OPENING HOURS

Banking hours are usually Monday-Friday 10am-4pm. Most banks in Dublin remain open until 5pm on Thursday and nearly all are open at lunchtime. Later closing times are gradually being introduced throughout Ireland.

Shops and **department stores** in Dublin are normally open Monday-Saturday 9am/9:30am-5:30/6pm. Late-night shopping is on Thursday when many shops stay open until 8pm. Some suburban shopping centres stay open until 9pm Thursday or Friday.

Post office branches are open Monday-Friday 9am-5:30pm, and Saturday 9am-1pm. The General Post Office in O'Connell Street is open until 8pm Monday-Saturday and 10:30am-6pm on Sunday and public holidays.

Museums and **Galleries** generally open Tuesdays-Saturdays 10am-5/6pm. Opening hours are shorter on Sundays, usually 2-5pm. The National Gallery is open seven days a week.

Pubs are open Monday-Saturday 10:30am-11:30pm and Sunday 12:30-2pm, 4-11:30pm. In the winter, evening closing time is 11pm.

PHOTOGRAPHY

All makes of film are easily found and can be developed overnight or even within an hour if need be. Airport security machines use X-rays, which can fog your film after more than four scannings. To be safe, ask the officer to check it by hand.

POLICE

Irish police (*Gardai*) can be recognized by their dark blue uniforms. An individual officer is called a *Garda Siochana* (guardian of the peace). In an emergency, dial **999** and ask for the police.

PUBLIC HOLIDAYS

Shops, banks, official departments, and restaurants are closed on public holidays. If a holiday falls on a Sunday, the following Monday is normally taken instead. Although Good Friday is not officially a public holiday, it is observed as such in most of Ireland.

1 January	*New Year's Day*
17 March	*St. Patrick's Day*

Dublin

| 25 December | *Christmas Day* |
| 26 December | *Boxing Day* |

Movable Dates

last weekend in May/	*Good Friday/Easter Monday*
first weekend in June	*Whit or June Holiday*
beginning of August	*August Holiday*
31 October or 1 November	*October Holiday (All Souls)*

 R

RELIGION

Ireland is predominantly a Roman Catholic country, but other non-Christian religions are represented in Dublin. For a list of services, ask at your hotel or look in the Saturday edition of the *Irish Times*.

Church of Ireland	Christ Church Cathedral, Edward Square; tel. 677 8099 St. Patrick's Cathedral, Patrick Street; tel. 453 9472
Roman Catholic	Pro-Cathedral, Marlborough Street; tel. 874 5441 University Church, 87a St. Stephen's Green; tel. 478 0616
Methodist	Dublin Central Mission, Abbey Street; tel. 874 0691
Jewish	Adelaide Road Synagogue, 37 Adelaide Road; tel. 676 1734
Muslim	Mosque and Islamic Centre, 163 South Circular Road, Dublin 8; tel. 454 3242

 T

TIME DIFFERENCES

Ireland follows Greenwich Mean Time (1 hour earlier than Central European Time) from November to March and British summer time (the same as Central European Time) from April to October.

New York	London	**Dublin**	Jo'burg	Sydney	Auckland
7am	noon	**noon**	2pm	10pm	12pm

TIPPING

Since a 15% service charge is normally included in hotel and restaurant bills, tipping is not obligatory unless service has been exceptional. If you're not sure whether a service charge has been added, ask. It's appropriate to give something extra to porters, cloakroom attendants, etc., for their services. The following are suggestions as to how much to leave.

Hairdresser/barber	10%
Porter, per bag	50p-IR£1
Taxi driver	10%
Tourist guide	10-15%

TOILETS/RESTROOMS

Dublin is not well provided with public conveniences, and you'll be better off using the facilities in museums, department stores, or pubs. Toilets may be labelled with symbols of a man or a woman, or with the words *Fir* for gentlemen and *Mna* for ladies.

TOURIST INFORMATION OFFICES

The **Irish National Tourist Board** — *Bord Fáilte* (literally "Board of Welcomes") — can inform you about when to go, where to stay, and what to see in Ireland and Dublin. Their head office is at Baggot Street Bridge, Dublin 2; tel. 602 4000, fax 602 4100. They also maintain offices in many countries throughout the world:

Canada: 160 Bloor Street East, Suite 1150, Toronto, Ontario M4W 1B9; tel. (416) 929 2777, fax (416) 929 6783

UK: 150 New Bond Street, London W1Y 0AQ; tel. (0171) 493 3201, fax (0171) 493 9065

USA: 345 Park Avenue, New York, NY 10154; tel. (212) 418 0800, fax (212) 371 9052

In the UK you can also contact **All Ireland Tourism**, 12 Regent Street, London SW1Y 4PQ; tel. (0171) 839 8416, fax 839 6179.

Dublin

On arrival, you can pick up a wealth of leaflets, brochures, and maps at **Dublin Tourism** offices located at the following addresses:

Arrivals Building, Dublin International Airport;
tel. 284 4768, fax 842 5886
14 Upper O'Connell Street, Dublin 1; tel. 284 4768, fax 284 1751
St. Michael's Wharf, Dun Laoghaire; tel. 284 4768, fax 842 5886

TRANSPORT

Bus

The city's **bus** network is operated by Dublin Bus-Bus Átha Cliath, which is a subsidiary of the national transport company CIE. Their distinctive, two-tone green, single- and double-deckers serve the city and the Greater Dublin area, including parts of Wicklow, Kildare, and Meath. Bus stops are frequent, and destinations and bus numbers are indicated at the front of the bus above the driver's window.

New bus services include CitySwift (white and blue single-decker buses) and Imp (yellow and red mini buses) on some routes.

An Lar means "City Centre," to which service is regular and efficient, with buses running from 6am-11:30pm, with a special hourly Nitelink service to the suburbs midnight-3am on Friday and Saturday (buses depart from College, D'Olier, and Westmoreland streets every hour). A frequent bus service links Heuston Station and Busaras with Dublin airport. You need to have the right change ready unless you have a special pass (see below), which should be inserted into the validator as you enter the bus on the right hand side (combined bus/DART tickets should be shown to the driver/conductor).

Rail/Dart

Dublin Area Rapid Transit (DART) provides a swift and efficient electrified **rail** link between the seaside towns of Howth in the north and Bray in the south. The line runs along the Dublin Bay coast and serves a total of 25 stations. Trains run approximately every 15 minutes (every 5 minutes during rush hours) 7am-midnight Monday-Saturday, and 9:30am-11pm Sunday. Avoid travelling at peak times when trains tend to be packed with commuters.

There are no flat fares on public transport, and the amount you pay depends on where you want to go, up to a maximum fare of IR£1.60. However, Dublin Bus offers a range of **discount passes** which are valid for bus or combined bus and rail and which make public transport much more economical for frequent travellers. The *one-day adult bus ticket* (IR£3.30) allows unlimited travel for one day on all Dublin Bus services (except Nitelink). The *one-day bus/rail ticket* (IR£4.50) allows unlimited transport on Dublin Bus and DART for one person (except on Nitelink) for one day, while the *family one-day ticket* (IR£6) extends the same concessions to two adults and up to four children under 16. The *Dublin Explorer Ticket* (IR£10) is valid for four consecutive days on bus and DART after 9:45am Monday-Friday, with no weekend restrictions. *Seven-day passes* are also available for unlimited travel, commencing on a Sunday (photo identification is required). Passes can be obtained from the Dublin Bus booking office at 59 O'Connell Street or from any bus ticket agent.

Taxi

The best place to get a **taxi** in Dublin is at one of the many clearly marked taxi ranks located outside major hotels, at bus and train stations and along St. Stephen's Green, O'Connell Street, and other busy thoroughfares. You'll rarely see taxis cruising for business.

Taxis are identified by a sign giving the name of the firm and their number on the car roof. Rates are fixed by law and displayed in all taxis. They are valid for a 16 km (10-mile) radius outside the city; beyond that, fares should be negotiated in advance with the driver.

You can arrange for a taxi by calling a specific company; look in the Golden Pages of the telephone directory under "Taxicabs." You will probably have to pay a pick-up charge if you order a taxi by phone.

Dublin

TRAVELLING TO DUBLIN

By Air

Ireland's national airline is Aer Lingus, which operates daily direct flights to Dublin from many airports in Britain and, in the United States, from Boston and New York. Ireland's other national airline, Ryanair, operates flights to Dublin (and other regional airports) from Stansted, Birmingham, Glasgow, Liverpool, and Manchester. Most other major airlines fly to Dublin, and principal air connections from continental Europe include services from Amsterdam, Brussels, Copenhagen, Düsseldorf, Frankfurt, Lisbon, Madrid, Milan, Munich, Paris, Rennes, Rome, and Zurich.

There is a wide range of special promotional fares to Ireland, and discounts are available for senior citizens, children, and students holding a valid International Student Identity Card. The cheapest fares on regular flights are APEX (advance purchase excursion) and super APEX, which must be booked and paid for three to four weeks in advance. Unless you leave things until the last minute, you will probably be able to book a charter flight or package including a hotel room, generally at rates and conditions even more reasonable than APEX. A wide range of inclusive package tours or special interest holidays are available, including fly-drive, sporting and activity holidays, and short breaks. Discuss your plans carefully with a reliable travel agent who should advise you on the best deals.

By Bus

Bus services linking Britain and Dublin are operated by Irish Ferries in conjunction with National Express in the UK, and with B&I and Sealink ferries. Supabus routes connect London and other major British towns to Dublin's central bus station, Busaras. Most routes run daily, but some are seasonal so you should contact your travel agent for the latest information.

Irish Ferries has a countrywide network of long-distance buses serving all cities and most towns and villages outside the Dublin area. All departures from Busaras (central bus station) in Store Street.

By Ferry
The most convenient passenger ferry services from Britain are between Holyhead and Dublin with B&I Line or between Holyhead and Dun Laoghaire (about 12.5 km/8 miles south of Dublin) with Stena Sealink Line. Stena Sealink also operates a catamaran service from Holyhead to Dun Laoghaire with an average crossing time of 1½ hours as well as a high-speed catamaran service. The Isle of Man Steam Packet Company offers a seasonal service (mid-May to mid-September) between Douglas and Dublin and also uses a catamaran. Irish Ferries sail from Roscoff to Cork and from Le Havre and Cherbourg to Rosslare.

By Rail
InterCity Ireland, operated by British Rail, runs a fast through-rail service connecting the whole of England and Scotland to all UK ports for onward shipping services to Ireland. This service connects via Irish Rail to stations throughout Ireland.

Bargain Saver and Family Fares are offered from British Rail stations to Irish Rail stations via Holyhead, Fishguard, and Stranraer. Full details of fares and services can be obtained from travel agents or from railway travel centres.

Listed below are several of the "go-as-you-please" passes available, best purchased in advance of travelling. The **InterRail Pass** for those under 26 and the **InterRail 26+ Pass** allow unlimited second-class travel on European rail networks within a defined number of countries and for a fixed period of time (1 month or 15 days). The **Freedom Pass** is available for travel on 3, 5, or 10 days within any month in one or more of 25 European countries. The **Rail-Europ-S card** gives seniors a 30% discount off journeys in more than one European country. Most passes are open to all nationalities.

WEIGHTS and MEASURES

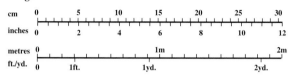

Length

| cm | 0 | 5 | 10 | 15 | 20 | 25 | 30 |
| inches | 0 | 2 | 4 | 6 | 8 | 10 | 12 |

| metres | 0 | 1m | 2m |
| ft./yd. | 0 | 1ft. | 1yd. | 2yd. |

Weight

| grams | 0 | 100 | 200 | 300 | 400 | 500 | 600 | 700 | 800 | 900 | 1kg |
| ounces | 0 | 4 | 8 | 12 | 1lb | 20 | 24 | 28 | 2lb |

Temperature

| °C | -30 | -25 | -20 | -15 | -10 | -5 | 0 | 5 | 10 | 15 | 20 | 25 | 30 | 35 | 40 | 45 |
| °F | -20 | -10 | 0 | 10 | 20 | 30 | 40 | 50 | 60 | 70 | 80 | 90 | 100 | 110 |

WOMEN TRAVELLERS

Women's Aid, PO Box 791, Dublin 7; tel. freefone 1800, 860 0033.
YWCA, 64 Lower Baggot Street, Dublin 2 (hostel), tel. 660 8452;
49 St. John's Road, Dublin 4; tel. 269 4521.

YOUTH HOSTELS

The Dublin International Youth Hostel in Mountjoy Street is a few minutes' walk from O'Connell Street on the north side of the Liffey. The hostel is open 24 hours a day and has storage lockers, an information desk, and restaurant and self-catering facilities. It is also the headquarters of the Irish Youth Hostels' Association (*An Oige*). For further information, contact them at 61 Mountjoy Street, Dublin 7; tel. 830 4555; website http://www.irelandyha.org.

A SELECTION
OF HOTELS
AND RESTAURANTS

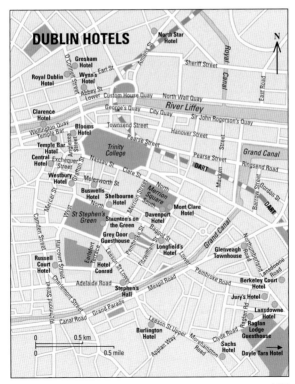

DUBLIN HOTELS

N

North Star Hotel

Amiens St

Sheriff Street

Royal Canal

East Road

Gresham Hotel

Earl St

Royal Dublin Hotel

O'Connell Street

Wynn's Hotel

Abbey St Lower

Custom House Quay

North Wall Quay

Clarence Hotel

George's Quay

City Quay

Sir John Rogerson's Quay

River Liffey

Wellington Quay

Aston Quay

Blooms Hotel

Townsend Street

Hanover Street

Temple Bar

Temple Bar Hotel

Pearse Street

Central Hotel

Exchequer Street

Anglesea St

Nassau St

Trinity College

Clare St

Pearse Street

Grand Canal

Ringsend Road

DART

Westbury Hotel

Grafton Street

Molesworth St

Merrion Square North

Merrion Street

DART

Mercer St

Buswells Hotel

Shelbourne Hotel

South

Mont Clare Hotel

Macken St

Barrow Street

Gordon St

St Stephen's Green

North

Staunton's on the Green

Davenport Hotel

Baggot St

Camden Street

Grey Door Guesthouse

Pembroke St

Fitzwilliam St

Longfield's Hotel

Glenveagh Townhouse

Northumberland Road

Lansdowne Road

Russell Court Hotel

Earlsfort Terrace

Leeson St Lower

Hotel Conrad

Pembroke Road

Berkeley Court Hotel

Harcourt Street

Charlemont Street

Adelaide Road

Stephen's Hall

Mespil Road

Jury's Hotel

Richmond Street

Canal Road

Grand Parade

Leeson St Upper

Grand Canal

Raglan Rd

Lansdowne Hotel

Clyde Road

Raglan Lodge Guesthouse

Burlington Hotel

Morehampton Road

Sachs Hotel

Appian Way

Doyle Tara Hotel

0   0.5 km

0   0.5 mile

Recommended Hotels

The standard of service in hotels and guesthouses can vary considerably, but those listed here should be satisfactory. Remember too that there is sometimes little difference between hotels and guesthouses, but the latter are usually cheaper, and that city centre hotels are usually more noisy. Many hotels advertise special offers in the *Irish Times*.

Listed below is a selection of hotels in four price categories, grouped in the following areas: Dublin City centre, south (suburbs), north (suburbs), and south coast. Although the tourist information offices at Dublin Airport and O'Connell Street both have hotel booking facilities, you are advised to book your accommodation well in advance, either through a travel agent or directly with the hotel. We have included telephone and fax numbers.

Breakfast and a service charge are normally *excluded* from the price of the room, and some establishments charge more during special events. As a basic guide to room prices, we have used the following symbols (for a double room with bath or shower, *including* breakfast, service charge, and tax):

✪✪✪✪	above IR£155
✪✪✪	IR£115-155
✪✪	IR£65-115
✪	below IR£65

CITY CENTRE

Blooms Hotel ✪✪✪ *6 Anglesea Street, Dublin 2; Tel. 671 5622, fax 671 5997.* A hotel with 86 rooms in the Temple Bar area, each with garment press and hair dryer. Restaurant, bar, basement nightclub. Car park.

Buswells Hotel ✪✪✪ *Molesworth Street, Dublin 2; Tel. 676 4013, fax 676 2090.* Centrally located (opposite the National Museums complex), set in a former Georgian townhouse with much period furniture. Rooms are all en suite. Restaurant and bars. Recently refurbished. Conference facilities.

Castle Hotel ✪ *3/4 Gardiner Row, Dublin 1; Tel. 874 6949, fax 872 7674.* A fine restored Georgian building, close to Parnell Square. En suite rooms with phone, TV. Car park. Recently refurbished.

Central Hotel ✪✪-✪✪✪ *1–5 Exchequer Street, Dublin 2; Tel. 679 7302, fax 679 7303.* A comfortable, refurbished Victorian building in a central location, with dining room and bars. Rooms include hair dryer, garment press and tea/coffee facilities.

Clarence Hotel ✪✪✪-✪✪✪✪ *6-8 Wellington Quay, Dublin 2; Tel. 670 9000, fax 670 7800.* Centrally located adjacent to Temple Bar, overlooking the River Liffey. Restaurant, nightclub and lift. All of the 50 rooms are en suite, and are uniquely designed.Recently renovated.

International Dublin Conrad ✪✪✪✪ *Earlsfort Terrace, Dublin 2; Tel. 676 5555, fax 676 5424.* Situated just off St. Stephen's Green, this glass construction opposite the National Concert Hall has 191 furnished, air-conditioned rooms, all with minibar, colour TV, clock radio, hair dryer, desk, and telephone. Two restaurants, a pub, and full business and conference facilities. Car park.

Davenport Hotel ✪✪✪✪ *Merrion Square, Dublin 2; Tel. 661 6800, fax 661 5663.* An elegant lemon-coloured building dating from the 1860s and set in a prime location. En suite rooms have TV, telephones, safe, hair dryer, garment press. Restaurant, bar, car park. All air-conditioned.

Gresham Hotel ✪✪✪✪ *23 Upper O'Connell Street, Dublin 1; Tel. 874 6881, fax 878 7175.* Some 200 en suite rooms with colour TV, telephone, garment press, hair dryer, and radio. Restaurant and

three bars. Fine, early 19th-century building in heart of city.
Meeting rooms and car park.

Grey Door Guesthouse ✪✪ *22-23 Upper Pembroke Street, Dublin 2; Tel. 676 3286, fax 676 3287,* A recently restored, elegant, and comfortable Georgian townhouse in harmonious surroundings near Fitzwilliam Square. Modern amenities include garment press, hair dryer, and tea/coffee facilities in each room. Excellent service.

Jury's Christchurch Inn ✪✪ *Christchurch Place, Dublin 8; Tel. 454 0000, fax 454 0012.* With an excellent location in the cathedral and castle area of the city (and situated directly opposite Christ Church), this new hotel is geared more for families, with comfortable accommodation at a reasonable price. All rooms are en suite and there is a restaurant bar, and car park.

Longfield's Hotel ✪✪-✪✪✪ *9/10 Lower Fitzwilliam Street, Dublin 2; Tel. 676 1367, fax 676 1542.* An excellent location in a splendid Georgian building near Merrion and Fitzwilliam squares characterizes this hotel. Lots of antique furniture and very well-appointed throughout. First-class restaurant.

Mont Clare Hotel ✪✪✪-✪✪✪✪ *Merrion Square, Dublin 2; Tel. 661 6799, fax 661 5663.* Conveniently located, an elegant hotel occupying a Georgian building. All rooms are air-conditioned, with hair dryer and garment press. Restaurant and bar. Car park.

North Star Hotel ✪✪ *Amiens Street, Dublin 1; Tel. 836 3136, fax 836 3561.,* A pleasant and well-run hotel in the city centre, close to O'Connell Station. All rooms have TV, radio, and telephone. Car park.

Royal Dublin Hotel ✪✪ *40 Upper O'Connell Street, Dublin 1; Tel. 873 3666, fax 873 3120.* Convenient central location near Parnell Square, a modern hotel with an old world ambience, with its own restaurant and bars, 117 en suite rooms. Car park.

Russell Court Hotel ✪✪ *Harcourt Street, Dublin 2; Tel. 478 4066, fax 478 1576.* Two Georgian houses make up this hotel of some 33 en suite modern-style rooms, each with TV and telephone. Harcourt Street runs south from St. Stephen's Green. Restaurant and bar.

Shelbourne Hotel ✪✪✪✪ *27 St. Stephen's Green, Dublin 2; Tel. 676 6471, fax 661 6006.* Dublin's most famous hotel and certainly one of its most distinctive, with art deco Egyptian lamp-holders outside. An excellent but noisy location. Plenty of antique furniture, a very good restaurant and bar, and a favourite place to meet for afternoon tea. Meeting rooms and car park.

Staunton's on the Green Guesthouse ✪✪-✪✪✪ *83 St. Stephen's Green, South Dublin 2; Tel. 478 2300, fax 478 2263.* Exclusive Georgian house overlooking the green, very comfortably appointed, and with splendid high ceilings and windows. All rooms en suite with telephone.

Temple Bar Hotel ✪✪-✪✪✪ *Fleet Street, Temple Bar, Dublin 2; Tel. 677 3333, fax 677 3088.* One of the city's newest hotels in a central location, a stone's throw away from Grafton Street. En suite rooms with TV, radio, hair dryer. Restaurant and bar.

Westbury Hotel ✪✪✪✪ *Grafton Street, Dublin 2; Tel. 679 1122, fax 679 7078.* A luxury city centre hotel, with 203 en suite rooms with telephone and TV. Restaurants and bars, conference and business facilities, car park, and shops.

Wynn's Hotel ✪✪ *35/39 Lower Abbey Street, Dublin 1; Tel. 874 5131, fax 874 1556.* This city centre hotel, just around the corner from the Abbey Theatre, has 68 en suite rooms with TV and telephone. Car Parking.

SOUTH OF THE CENTRE

Anglesea Town House ✪✪ *63 Anglesea Road, Ballsbridge, Dublin 4; Tel. 668 3877, fax 668 3461.* This Edwardian guesthouse offers seven rooms, all with shower, TV, and telephone, and every home comfort in pleasant Ballsbridge.

Berkeley Court Hotel ✪✪✪✪ *Lansdowne Road, Dublin 4; Tel. 660 1711, fax 661 7238.* A sumptuously appointed hotel. All 190 rooms have en suite bathroom, colour TV, radio, and telephone. Restaurant, coffee shop, and bar. Gym, sauna, and shops. Car park.

Dublin

Burlington Hotel ✪✪✪✪ *Upper Leeson Street, Dublin 4; Tel. 660 5222, fax 660 8496.* An extremely well-appointed hotel with 451 rooms, all with en suite bathroom, colour TV, radio, and telephone. Restaurants, nightclub (can be noisy), and shops. Conference facilities and car park.

Doyle Montrose Hotel ✪✪✪ *Stillorgan Road, Dublin 4; Tel. 269 3311, fax 269 1164.* All 179 rooms in this modern hotel have their own bathroom, TV, and telephone. Also in the hotel: restaurants and bar, shop, conference rooms, and car park.

Doyle Tara Hotel ✪✪✪ *Merrion Road, Dublin 4; Tel. 269 4666, fax 269 1027.* A modern building overlooking Dublin Bay, that is very convenient for ferry port and public transport to the city. All 114 rooms with bathroom, colour TV, telephone. Two restaurants, bar, shop. Car park.

Glenveagh Townhouse ✪-✪✪ *31 Northumberland Road, Ballsbridge, Dublin 4; Tel. 668 4612, fax 668 4559.* A pleasant Victorian house offering 10 en suite rooms, all equipped with TV and telephone. Lovely windows and ceilings and in a quiet location.

Hibernian Hotel ✪✪✪-✪✪✪ *Eastmoreland Place, Ballsbridge, Dublin 4; Tel. 668 7666, fax 660 2655.* A secluded, traditionally furnished hotel with all modern amenities in elegant surroundings.

Jury's Hotel ✪✪✪-✪✪✪✪ *Penbroke Road, Ballsbridge, Dublin 4; Tel. 660 5000, fax 660 5540.* Large, international hotel with 300 deluxe rooms and 100 super deluxe rooms. Two restaurants, 22½ hour Coffee Dock Grill, bar, and swimming pool. Car park. Relaxed atmosphere; families welcomed. Famous evening cabaret.

Lansdowne Hotel ✪✪-✪✪✪ *27-29 Pembroke Road, Ballsbridge, Dublin 4; Tel. 668 2522, fax 668 5585.* Set back from a tree-lined road in Ballsbridge, offering 40 en suite rooms with telephone, TV, and radio. Restaurant, bar, and car park.

Mount Herbert Guesthouse ✪ *Herbert Road, Landsdowne*

Road, Dublin 4; Tel. 668 4321, fax 660 7077. A large, extended Victorian building with car park and children's play area, near Lansdowne Road DART. Some 135 functional but comfortable en suite rooms with TV, telephone, and garment press. Good value, but rather brusque service. Can be noisy, so ask for a quiet room.

Raglan Lodge Guesthouse ✪✪ *10 Raglan Road, Ballsbridge, Dublin 4; Tel. 660 6697, fax 660 6781.* A splendid Victorian house situated in the leafy suburb of Ballsbridge, this extremely well-run accommodation comprises seven en suite rooms with TV, telephone, and tea/coffee facilities. Private parking also available.

Sachs Hotelm ✪✪-✪✪✪ *19–29 Morehampton Road, Donnybrook, Dublin 4; Tel. 668 0995, fax 668 6147.* All en suite rooms are equipped with their own TV and telephone. This pleasurant building also comprises a leisure centre and nightclub, and is characterized by a good standard of service. Car park.

Stephens Hall ✪✪✪-✪✪✪✪ *The Earlsfort Centre, Lower Leeson Street, Dublin 2; Tel. 661 0585, fax 661 0606.* This is an all-suite hotel set in a row of Georgian terraced houses. It is particularly suitable for an extended stay. The suites comprise a small kitchen, dining area, sitting room, bathroom, and one or two bedrooms. There is a restaurant, and car parking is also available.

NORTH OF THE CENTRE

Doyle Skylon Hotel ✪✪✪ *Drumcondra Road, Dublin 9; Tel. 837 9121, fax 837 2778.* A modern building situated in a convenient location for the airport (on the busy main road into the city centre). All 92 en suite rooms have TV, radio, and telephone. There are two restaurants, bars, shops; also meeting rooms and car park.

Egans Guesthouse ✪ *7/9 Iona Park, Glasnevin, Dublin 9; Tel. 830 3611, fax 830 3312.* This is a very pleasant Victorian residence in a similar neighbourhood. It is a little out of the way, north of the city centre and near the splendid botanic gardens.

There are 23 en suite rooms with phone, TV, and tea/coffee facilities. Car park.

Forte Posthouse ✪✪✪ *Airport Road, Dublin Airport, Co. Dublin; Tel. 844 4211, fax 844 6002.* An airport hotel designed for a brief stay (a courtesy coach shuttles visitors between the airport and the hotel all day long). There are restaurants, bars, meeting rooms, and car park. All rooms have hair dryer, garment press, and tea/coffee facilities.

SOUTH COAST

The Court Hotel ✪✪-✪✪✪ *Killiney Bay Road, Killiney, Co. Dublin; Tel. 285 1622, fax 285 2085.* All 86 rooms have a telephone and TV in this Victorian hotel, overlooking Dublin Bay and adjacent to a DART station. There is a restaurant and a coffee shop, as well as meeting rooms and a car park. The hotel offers good old-fashioned service.

Fitzpatrick Castle Hotel ✪✪✪ *Killiney Hill Road, Killiney, Co. Dublin; Tel. 284 0700, fax 285 0207.* Situated in its own 3.5-ha (9-acre) grounds 14.5 km (9 miles) south of the city centre (with courtesy bus). All 90 en suite rooms have TV, phone, and radio. Restaurant, bar, sporting facilities. Friendly service. Conference facilities. Car park.

Kingston Hotel ✪✪-✪✪✪ *Adelaide Street (088 Georges Street), Seafront Dun Laoghaire, Co. Dublin; Tel. 280 1810, fax 280 1237.* Overlooking Dublin Bay and convenient for ferryport and train services. Modern-style furniture with all amenities. All rooms en suite. Restaurant. Nightclub.

Royal Marine Hotel ✪✪-✪✪✪ *Marine Road, Dun Laoghaire, Co. Dublin; Tel. 280 1911, fax 280 1089.* With 1.5-hectare (4-acre) gardens on the seafront overlooking Dublin Bay, a fully restored and renovated Victorian building with a new wing. All 99 en suite rooms have TV, telephone, garment press, and hair dryer. Meeting rooms, car park. Golf.

Recommended Restaurants

Dublin has a superb range of both traditional Irish and cosmopolitan restaurants. Most offer both *table d'hôte* and *à la carte* menus. With the former you pay a fixed price for a set three- or four-course lunch or dinner, whereas *à la carte* offers a choice of individually priced dishes. Meal prices include 12.5% government tax, and a 15% service charge is usually added to the final bill. Several restaurants in Dublin participate in the tourist menu scheme, offering a small selection of set price menus at a reasonable price. Alternatively, economical pub lunches are offered by most pubs in Dublin.

Look for special offers in the *Irish Times* and local press, and remember also that many museums and other attractions have fine cafés of their own. Vegetarians are very well catered to and no matter what you like, you should be able to find something to suit your taste. Remember that some restaurants are closed on Monday.

As a basic guide, the following symbols give an idea of the price for a three-course meal for one, including a service charge of 10-15% but excluding wine (drinks, of course, can add considerably to the final bill):

✿✿✿	above IR£15
✿✿	IR£10-15
✿	below IR£10

CITY CENTRE NORTH

Chapter One Restaurant ✿✿-✿✿✿ *18/19 Parnell Square, Dublin 1; Tel. 873 2266/873 2281.* Under the same management as the Old Dublin Restaurant (see page 138), this establishment, in the basement of the Dublin Writers Museum, has quickly established itself as one of the city's best. Excellent dishes are accompanied by fine wines. The restaurant is open for lunches (12-2:30pm, Mon-Fri) and dinners (6-11pm, Tues-Sat), and pre-theatre menus are available from 6pm. Reservations advised.

101 Talbot ✪✪-✪✪✪ *101-102 Talbot Street (Upstairs), Dublin 1; Tel. 874 5011.* Do not let the unprepossessing appearance of Talbot Street put you off this excellent restaurant. Superb international food is served in generous portions by a friendly staff at very reasonable prices, and there is a good wine list. A relaxed atmosphere attracts a wide range of people: come early for lunch and book for dinner. Open 10am-11pm Tues.–Sat.

The Winding Stair ✪ *40 Lower Ormond Quay, Dublin 1; Tel. 873 3292.* A café and a bookshop with fine views over the River Liffey. It has a good reputation but can be inconsistent in quality and also becomes crowded. An emphasis on salads, soups, and breads attracts the alternative set, and it's not called the Winding Stair for nothing. Open 10:30am-6pm.

OLD TOWN/LIBERTIES

Les Frères Jacques ✪✪✪ *74 Dame Street, Dublin 2; Tel. 679 4555.* Seconds away from the Olympia Theatre and Dublin Castle, you can eat authentic French cuisine in this small upstairs restaurant, in a relaxed and informal atmosphere and agreeable surroundings. Lots of meat and fish dishes and delicious sauces. Open 12:30-2:30pm, 7-10.:30pm.

Old Dublin Restaurant ✪✪-✪✪✪ *90/91 Francis Street, Dublin 8; Tel. 454 2028/454 2346.* Specializing in Russian and Scandinavian recipes such as *borscht*, *novgorod* (beef chateaubriand with fried barley and caviar), and *pelmini* (small beef or veal dumplings in consommé), and using only fresh Irish produce, this unusual but long-established restaurant will set you up for antique hunting in Francis Street. Open 12:30-2:30pm, 6-11pm. Book in advance.

TEMPLE BAR

Elephant and Castle ✪-✪✪ *18 Temple Bar, Dublin 2; Tel.*

679 3121. The relaxed informality of the staff and premises as well as the excellent food have made this the most popular informal restaurant in the city. If you crave a selection of quality burgers and salads, and meals with more than a hint of Mexican or Thai influence, this is the place. Vegetarian options, licensed. Open 8am-12pm.

Gallagher's Boxty House ✪-✪✪ *20-21 Temple Bar, Dublin 2; Tel. 677 2762.* Traditional Irish food is served here, including boxty, a potato pancake stuffed with a variety of fillings (including vegetarian). Plain food at plain prices, served to traditional Irish music, means the place is very popular. Open noon-11pm.

Irish Film Centre Restaurant ✪ *6 Eustace Street, Temple Bar, Dublin 2; Tel. 677 0879.* Widely acclaimed for its food and pleasant surroundings, the film centre restaurant serves daily lunch specials and sandwiches with an emphasis on freshness. Vegetarian options are available, and the cakes have to be eaten to be believed. Bar licence. Open 12:30-8:30pm Sun-Tues, 12:30-11pm Wed-Sat.

Omar Khayyam ✪-✪✪ *51 Wellington Quay, Temple Bar, Dublin 2; Tel. 677 5758.* On the north side of Temple Bar by the Ha'penny Bridge, this small corner restaurant offers a vast range of Middle Eastern dishes like falafels, cous cous, and pita breads with a variety of fillings. Vegetarian options abound, and the establishment has a wine licence. Open noon-midnight.

Well Fed Café ✪ *Dublin Resource Centre, 6 Crow Street, Dublin 2; Tel. 677 2234.* This is an award-winning vegetarian restaurant (a workers' co-operative) which serves excellent food in generous portions at very cheap prices. Relaxed and very bohemian — it feels rather like sitting in a workers' canteen — it always offers a range of specials. Children welcome. Open 12:30-8:30pm.

CITY CENTRE SOUTH

Bewley's Oriental Café ✪ *Branches in Grafton Street, Westmoreland Street, Mary Street, South Great George's Street.*

Dublin

The food and drink are overpriced, but you come here to watch people and to experience something important about Dublin, particularly in the faded Grafton Street branch, where there is also occasional theatre, poetry, and dance on late-night weekends. The new Mary Street Bewley's is cleaner and more cheerful. Open 7:30am-1am.

The Bistro ✪✪ *4 & 5 Castle Market, Dublin 2; Tel. 671 5430.* A young and informal Italian restaurant which serves a wide range of excellent dishes all day. Friendly service, and children are welcome (pens and colouring books provided). Open daily 8am-12pm (2am Fri, Sat).

Blazing Salads ✪ *Powerscourt Townhouse Centre (2nd floor), Clarendon Street, Dublin 2; Tel. 671 9552.* Delicious wholefood at tempting prices will tempt you back here every day, particularly if you require a vegetarian or other special diet. A wide range of salads accompanies hot dishes like vegetable moussaka or bean casserole. Good wines are also available in this relaxed eating house. Open 9:30am-6pm.

Break for the Border ✪✪ *Stephen's Stree, Dublin 2; Tel. 478 0300.* A Tex-Mex restaurant and bar that does a lot of business, with plenty of loud music to complement the loud and lively customers. Open noon-midnight.

Captain America's ✪✪ *Grafton Court, Grafton Street, Dublin 2; Tel. 671 5266.* If you're hankering after some good old American food served in a good old American restaurant, this is the place for you. Open noon-2:30am.

The Cedar Tree ✪✪-✪✪✪ *11a St. Andrew Street, Dublin 2; Tel. 677 2121.* This is Lebanese food at its best, the authentic stuff and reasonably priced. The decoration is suitably exotic (as are some of the customers) and the atmosphere totally unique, particularly on weekends when there is the added attraction of a belly dancer. In addition, vegetarians get a good meal. Open 5:30-11pm.

Chili Club ✪✪ *1 Anne's Lane, off South Anne Street, Dublin 2; Tel. 677 3721.* Thai cuisine at its best, served in a rather small, youthful and friendly restaurant that has become very popular (booking is therefore essential). Some vegetarian options on an otherwise extensive menu. Open for lunch and dinner Mon-Fri.

Chompys ✪ *Powerscourt Townhouse Centre (1st floor), Clarendon Street, Dublin 2; Tel. 679 4552.* The menu's terrible punning describes a beguiling range of American-deli food in the agreeable surroundings of the Powerscourt Townhouse. Toasted bagels, huge stacks of sandwiches, and an all- American breakfast served with coffee are the chief delights; there are also some wicked cakes to tempt you. Open 8am-6pm Mon-Sat (7pm Thurs).

The Commons ✪✪✪ *Newman House, 85/86 St. Stephen's Green South , Dublin 2; Tel. 475 2597/ 478 0530.* An extremely good basement restaurant with much fine Georgian architectural detail and a wonderful terrace garden. The service is excellent and the menu changes constantly, making this one of the best and most popular formal restaurants in Dublin. Open 12:30-2.15pm, 7-10pm.

Cornucopia ✪ *19 Wicklow Street, Dublin 2; Tel. 677 7583.* A small self-service vegetarian restaurant which offers delicious meals like Turkish bean casserole, heaps of tasty salads and wholemeal breads and rolls. Very good value and not to be missed. Open 9am-8pm Mon.-Sat.

Ernie's ✪✪✪ *Mulberry Gardens, Donnybrook, Dublin 4; Tel. 269 3300.* An interesting restaurant which is built around a mulberry tree, with the main dining room lined with contemporary Irish paintings. The cooking and presentation is classical, with charcoal grill, and seafood and game in season. Closed Sun.–Mon.

Fitzers Café ✪✪ *Branches at 24 Upper Baggot Street, National Gallery (Merrion Square West) , Royal Dublin Society and Dawson Street.* All the above-mentioned branches are stylishly cool cafés serving a range of international dishes and a selection of splendid cakes and tarts. Licensed, vegetarian options. Open 11am-11:30pm (except National Gallery branch, which has the same hours as the museum).

Galligan's ✪ *6 Merrion Row, Dublin 2; Tel. 676 5955.* A self-service restaurant and coffee shop serving salads and hot meals (vegetarian options also available), homemade cakes and pastries. The good food at good prices can be washed down with some of the attractive wines offered. Open 8am-7pm, Sat. 9am-5pm.

La Cave ✪✪ *South Anne Street, Dublin 2; Tel. 679 4409.* Dublin's oldest authentic French wine bar, open for lunch and dinner. Reasonably priced with excellent wine list. Open 12:30-11pm Mon.–Sat., 6-11pm Sun.

Marks Brothers ✪ *7 South Great Georges Street , Dublin 2; Tel. 677 1085.* Inexpensive, but the city-renowned sandwiches and homemade soups and salads, accompanied by rock music, attract a young student crowd for a quick lunch. Vegetarian options available. Open 10am-5pm.

Mitchell's Cellars ✪✪ *21 Kildare Street, Dublin 2; Tel. 668 0367.* This cellar wine bar, full of wine memorabilia from the emporium above, is open only for lunch, when its 60-odd tables are quickly occupied. If you arrive early you can enjoy the extensive if straightforward menu, and relax afterwards over a drink in order to soak up the unique atmosphere. Open 12.15-2:30pm.

O'Dwyer's ✪ *7 Lower Mount Street, Dublin 2; Tel. 676 1717.* O'Dwyer's proves that you can combine a traditional Irish pub with a pizzeria serving a wide range of Italian food, and that the result need not be expensive. Children are welcome and from 5-8pm you can have as much as you can eat from the pizza bar for around IR£5 per person. A convivial atmosphere does mean large lunchtime crowds, but you can at least drink without having to wait.

Pasta Fresca ✪✪ *3/4 Chatham Street, Dublin 2; Tel. 679 2402.* A popular and relaxed restaurant, serving, as the name suggests, virtually every possible combination of pasta and sauce plus some free helpings of salads. You could, if you wanted, have breakfast, lunch, and dinner in this very same place. Vegetarian options and licensed. Open 7:30am-11:30pm.

Patrick Guilbaud ✪✪✪ *46 St. James'sPlace, (off Lower Baggot Street), Dublin 2 ; Tel. 676 4192.* Difficult to locate, this restaurant serves superb French cuisine — at a price. It is slightly pretentious. Booking advised. Open 12:30-2pm, 7:30-10.15pm, closed Sun.

Periwinkle Seafood Bar ✪ *Powerscourt Townhouse Centre (ground floor) , 59 S. William Street, Dublin 2; Tel. 679 4203.* Yet another great source of food in the Powerscourt Townhouse. Excellent seafood makes it one of the city's most popular lunchtime cafés. The menu capitalizes on the day's local catch, with a delicious Periwinkle chowder; 11am-5pm.

Rajdoot Tandoori ✪✪-✪✪✪ *26–28 Clarendon Street , Dublin 2; Tel. 679 4280.* A superb award-winning Indian restaurant with a vast menu, much of which is suitable for vegetarians. Served in appropriately opulent surroundings and licensed. You haven't eaten Indian until you've eaten here. Open noon-2:30pm, 6:30-11:30pm.

Roly's Bistro ✪✪✪ *7 Ballsbridge Terrace, Dublin 4; Tel. 668 2611.* Attractive bistro restaurant on two floors, serving imaginative and well-presented lunch and dinner menus, usually focused around original fish and meat dishes. Although only a recent arrival, it has become immensely popular.

The Trocadero ✪✪-✪✪✪ *3 St. Andrew's Street, Dublin 2; Tel. 677 5545.* Very popular with media types (including those in front of the camera), who look for their own signed photographs on the walls. The reasonably priced food is competent but you really come here for the atmosphere. Vegetarian options. Open 6-12:30am.

SOUTH SUBURBS

Canaletto's ✪-✪✪ *69 Mespil Road, Dublin 4; Tel. 678 5084.* Tucked a little out of the way by the canal, this bizarrely decorated take-away and restaurant caters chiefly to a knowledgeable office crowd, anxious for adventurous sandwiches, salads, and hot dishes. Get there early. Vegetarian options. Open 8am-11pm.

Le Coq Hardi ✪✪✪ *35 Pembroke Road, Dublin 4; Tel. 668 4130/668 9070.* Extremely good French cuisine is served in this rather forbidding Ballsbridge townhouse. The formality of the service and the surroundings is more suited to dinner than lunch, but the place is always discreetly busy, its rich patrons attracted as much by the magnificent wine cellar as the food. Open 12:30-2:30pm, 7-11pm. Reservations recommended.

Jury's Coffee Dock ✪✪ *Jury's Hotel and Towers, Pembroke Road, Ballsbridge, Dublin 4; Tel. 660 5000.* The value of the Coffee Dock, especially if you are staying in the Ballsbridge area, is that you know you can have a good, reasonably priced meal or snack at virtually any time of day or night. Service is good and friendly, the range of dishes large (with vegetarian options) and it is licensed. Open 22½ hours a day.

Señor Sassi's ✪✪ *146 Upper Leeson Street, Dublin 4; Tel. 668 4544.* One of the city's most recent brasseries, Sassi's specializes in Middle Eastern and Mediterranean dishes. Versatile menu. Booking advised.

OUTSIDE DUBLIN

King Sitric ✪✪✪ *East Pier, Howth, Co. Dublin; Tel. 823 6729.* Named after the first king of Dublin, this restaurant, housed in a Georgian residence, has a good, if rather pricey reputation for seafood. Closed on Sun. Reservations recommended.

Restaurant na Mara ✪✪ *Dun Laoghaire Harbour, Co. Dublin; Tel. 280 6767/280 0509.* Although situated farther along the coast, this formal and quite expensive restaurant enjoys a fine reputation for fish dishes.